Curing ADD/ADHD Children

Curing ADD/ADHD Children

Peter T. Oas, Ph.D.

Pentland Press, Inc.
www.pentlandpressusa.com

PUBLISHED BY PENTLAND PRESS, INC.
5122 Bur Oak Circle, Raleigh, North Carolina 27612
United States of America
919-782-0281

ISBN 1-57197-272-2
Library of Congress Control Number: 2001 131180

Printed in the United States of America

This book is dedicated to my loving and supportive wife, Mya, who has taught me much about raising non-ADD children.

Table of Contents

Introduction . . . . *xv*

Chapter 1: ADD is Not a Medical Disorder or Disease *1*

Chapter 2: Medical Treatment for a Psychological Problem *15*

Chapter 3: Drugs for ADD *23*

Chapter 4: Money—In Research and Practice *37*

Chapter 5: ADD—A Social and Cultural Cure *47*

Chapter 6: Temperament and Resistance *61*

Chapter 7: Parenting Works *79*

Chapter 8: My Personal and Professional Experience *91*

Chapter 9: The Therapeutic Process *109*

Chapter 10: One Parent's Experience of Therapy *129*

Chapter 11: Bobby—Severe ADD *137*

Chapter 12: Mark—A Parent's Introspective Changes *147*

Chapter 13: Susie—ADD and Bipolar Disorder *151*

Chapter 14: John—Parent Anger and Marital Problems *157*

Chapter 15: Willie—Divorced Parents Working Together *165*

Chapter 16: Heather—ADD Parents *171*

Chapter 17: Lisa—Adjustment to Divorce *179*

Chapter 18: Conclusion *185*

Bibliography *189*

Foreword

An Inspired Approach at a Critical Time
Peter R. Breggin, M.D.

This book arrives at a critical time and offers an informed, inspired approach by a very experienced and dedicated psychologist.

At the present time approximately 6 million children in the United States are being diagnosed with Attention Deficit Hyperactivity Disorder (ADHD) and treated with stimulant drugs such as Ritalin (methylphenidate), Concerta (long-acting methylphenidate) and Adderall (amphetamine). If you are a parent, you run a high risk of being told by a teacher that your child has ADHD and needs medication. If you're a teacher, you've been encouraged to believe that many of your students could benefit from drugs. If you are a mental health professional, you feel pressured to go along with the widespread practice of psychiatrically diagnosing and medicating children.

Why should you raise a critical eye toward this common practice?

To begin with, ADHD is not a disease or a disorder in the ordinary sense of those words. ADHD is not a set of genuine symptoms that can be related to an underlying physical or psychological problem. ADHD was developed as a list of behaviors that disrupt classrooms. That is the only way to understand the kinds of behaviors listed in the official diagnosis as published in the American Psychiatric Association's Diagnostic and Statistical Manual of Mental Disorders, IV (1994). These behaviors include "squirms in seat," "often leaves seat," "often talks excessively," "does not seem to listen when spoken to directly," and "often blurts out answers before questions have been completed." Over a period of decades, drug advocates compiled a list of every behavior that requires extra attention in a classroom and lumped them together to make them look like a related disorder. As a result, almost any child who fails to be submissive or passive in the classroom can be fit into the ADHD diagnosis.

If ADHD is not a disorder, what is it? In fact, "it " is just what it seems to be - a list of potentially annoying or disruptive behaviors that make demands on adults. They occur when a child is in conflict with teachers, parents, or other authorities.

Why do children display ADHD-like behaviors? The reasons are infinite. Many of these children don't have any problems at all; the adults in their lives have unrealistic expectations. In my psychiatric practice, I often find that teachers expect too much conformity from a particular student or that their teaching techniques are uninspired, or that their classrooms are too large. These children are normal; the situations aren't meeting their needs or the adults have too limited a view of acceptable childhood behaviors.

Even when children seem extremely hyperactive or out of control, the environment is often the obvious source of the problem. A child who seems flagrantly "ADHD" in one classroom may seem calm and self-disciplined in another. Some children in my practice have been "cured" by transfer to another teacher or school. Similarly, a child who is drastically hyperactive with one parent will often be a model of good conduct with the other.

Many children also go through periods of time when, for no obvious reason, they don't feel comfortable in their classroom or home. Even when extreme, their rebellious and provocative behavior may turn out to be nothing more than a developmental stage that requires adult firmness and patience.

At other times, children will display ADHD-like behaviors because they are frustrated, unhappy, and anxious. Usually these painful feelings can be traced to problems in the home or school, such as conflicts in parenting, unrecognized educational needs, or peer abuse in the school or neighborhood.

What are the "cures" for ADHD-like behaviors? There is no alternative to getting to know each individual child, including the quality of the child's life in the home, school, and wider community of peers and adults. In my psychiatric practice, if a child is having problems in the home, I work with the parents to develop a proper balance of unconditional love and rational discipline. Individual parents are often inconsistent in their approaches, causing confusion in the child's mind. Sometimes one or both parents are suffering from emotional problems that are affecting the child. Commonly, the parents are in conflict with each other or have already separated. If the child is out of control at home, he or she will usually respond quickly to any improvements in the attitudes and actions of the parents.

If most of the problems occur at school rather than at home, then parenting may have little or nothing to do with it. The parents need to assess the teacher and the classroom, and also their child's approach to being in the school. Sometimes parents can help their children learn better ways to react in the classroom. Often, the teacher and the school need to pay more attention to the disciplinary needs of the child.

Is there ever a place for stimulant drugs in the treatment of ADHD-like behaviors? At the extreme, stimulants make many children robotic and submissive at the expense of their spirit. But even when the effects are subtle, the drugs work in the same way - by sufficiently stifling the child's energy, creativity, and overall mental life to bring about greater docility and conformity. Using drugs to make children more submissive and compliant is not a rational, ethical, or medically justified approach to improving a child's conduct or schoolwork. There is no place for drugging children in order to control their behavior or to make them conform to our expectations. The entire idea of giving stimulants for "ADHD" lacks scientific foundation and should be abandoned.

Not only does the ADHD diagnosis lack scientific validity, stimulant drugs are far more dangerous that most parents, teachers, or doctors realize. My books and articles review and scientifically document these adverse effects in great detail. The harmful effects include suppressing the child's physical development and mental growth, causing biochemical imbalances in the brain and permanently harming brain function; causing depression, anxiety, and psychosis; and predisposing the child to stimulant addiction and abuse in future years. A growing number of animal studies show that stimulant drugs cause permanent abnormalities in brain function and even the death of brain cells.

Not only are stimulant drugs dangerous, they are ineffective. Studies that claim to show benefits are usually limited to a few weeks in duration and simply confirm that the drugs can suppress behavior in many children for a few weeks. Despite years of trying, however, drug advocates have produced no convincing evidence that stimulant drugs improve the child's self-esteem or social life, or that they improve learning or educational achievement. In fact, the drugs narrow the child's focus by limiting the child's imagination and creativity. The willingness to do otherwise disagreeable tasks, such as homework, comes at the cost of impaired neurological and mental functioning.

As a psychiatric expert in legal cases and in my practice, I have evaluated children who are suffering from the toxic effects of three, four, or even five psychiatric drugs. Typically they are emotionally blunted and their behavior has deteriorated. As I gradually wean them from the drugs, and provide their parents counseling with me or with another professional, the child improves. The parents often report, "We have our child back." In retrospect, they are dismayed that they allowed teachers and doctors to push them to medicate their children instead of meeting their needs for improved parenting or schooling, including a balance of discipline, love, play and engaging education.

We cannot help our children by applying cookie cutter labels to them. We cannot help them by suppressing their brains and minds with dangerous drugs. There is no substitute for taking the time to figure out what is going on in the lives of individual children. And there is no substitute for providing them the adult resources needed while they are growing up and dependent upon us.

Psychologist Dr. Peter Oas has spent many years learning to identify and to successfully address the genuine problems of children. This book will benefit parents, teachers, therapists, and doctors who want to help children grow to fulfill their real potential as human beings.

Dr. Breggin is a psychiatrist in private practice in Bethesda, Maryland. He is the founder of the International Center for the Study of Psychiatry and Psychology and the author of many books and articles, including "Talking Back to Ritalin" (revised, 2001), "The Antidepressant Fact Book" (2001), and "Reclaiming Our Children" (2000).

Acknowledgements

The author wishes to acknowledge the gracious help he received in producing this book. To Susan Wyman for her assistance in typing and editing. To Wilma Weekly, Carol Phillips and Dr. Jon Brooks in their proofing and editorial help. To Carol Schoefield and Sue Carrigan for help in research and marketing. To all who offered reviews of the manuscript, some of whom are listed on the back cover. To Peter and Ginger Breggin for remaining steadfast in their advocacy work with children. I am especially grateful to all the parents and referral sources over the years whom have entrusted me with the care of their children, who had the strength to look past the popular and perseverance to resist the easy way out and not settle for less.

Introduction

(Growing up) is especially difficult to achieve for a child whose parents do not take him seriously; that is, who do not expect proper behavior from him, do not discipline him, and finally, do not respect him enough to tell him the truth.

—Thomas S. Szasz
(1972)

Children are wonderful. They can also be frustrating, demanding, irritating, disrespectful, inattentive, hyperactive, defiant, bored, disinterested, and lazy. Every parent experiences some, if not all, of these behaviors while trying to raise a child. Likewise, all teachers experience these behaviors in the classroom. The ramifications of these behaviors are dire. Teachers can spend more class time on discipline than on education. Society spends more money building juvenile detention facilities, and parents with their physicians spend more time and money sedating, restraining, subduing and suppressing their children than they do effectively communicating with them.

Living an organized, disciplined, healthy lifestyle is not easy for parents in today's high-speed, high-stress society. Therefore, it is not unusual to see unorganized, undisciplined, unhealthy children. What is unusual is what we as a society are doing with these children. We build even more juvenile detention facilities. We diagnose badly behaved children as "disabled" and allocate millions of dollars in Social Security disability for their care outside the home. We create special education programs for behavior-disordered children within the schools. We lock children up in inpatient psychiatric treatment centers. We drug our kids. None of these are solutions, as is evidenced by the increasingly serious and violent crimes committed by psychotropically medicated children every day or by beliefs that childrens behavior is incurable.

Mental health professionals diagnose unorganized, undisciplined, unattentive children with a condition known as attention deficit disorder (ADD/ADHD). However, there are seemingly as many theories about what causes ADD and how to treat this condition as there are children and parents who suffer with it. Some believe that ADD is a physiological reaction to environmental substances like lead, allergens, television, or too much sugar. They prescribe a nutritional supplement or diet change as a cure. Others believe that ADD is a reaction to social stressors like abuse, poverty, fast-paced modernism, or a poor educational system. This group recommends social changes as a solution. Still others believe that ADD is a brain disease or a form of brain damage from ineffective neurotransmission at receptor sites, damaged or poorly developed structures in the frontal lobes of the brain, or other general nervous system dysfunction, or even genetic abnormality. This camp dispenses drugs as an answer. Finally, some believe ADD is an inborn temperament trait, or maybe even an unappreciated gift causing the child to be a "social misfit." These individuals do not attempt to change ADD behavior, but to teach accommodation to life.

I do not subscribe to any of the above theories, but rather suggest that ADD is initially a normal part of the spectrum of developing human behavior. All one- and two-year-old children are ADD–they look, they feel, they touch, and they explore, sometimes inappropriately—and will continue to do so for the rest of their lives. Parents must teach their children to differentiate between those behaviors that are acceptable and those that are not. ADD then is a childhood behavioral response to parenting that does not control and shape children to be non-ADD. In short, I consider ADD to be the "terrible two's" unresolved. As such, I cannot fathom a cure for ADD that does not focus on effective parenting.

But parents sometimes do not have enough experience, skill, or energy to expend upon their children teaching them how to sit still, listen, reflect, or act constructively. Many parents can be so tired when they finally pick up their children at five or six o'clock from after-school care programs that they can barely feed the children and get them to bed. How much effective time do you actually spend teaching your child to behave correctly? Be honest.

The answer for most readers is simply not enough. The typical parent probably spends less than a few hours per week effectively communicating with his or her child about appropriate behavior. There is often not enough time to provide children with the consistent discipline necessary to establish non-ADD behavior patterns. Parents and enabling mental health professionals with ineffective theories are teaching their children to misbehave by default and creating an ADD epidemic.

Debate about the existence and power of human free will has waged since the dawn of scientific thought. Do we have a capacity to be self-directing or are we at the mercy of external or internal forces beyond our control? Philosopher Rene Descartes lamented, "Am I so dependent on the body and the senses that without these I cannot exist?" When Descartes later stated, "I think therefore I am,"a conceptual groundwork for the importance of thought relative to the senses and emotion, as a key to understanding, has been laid. Cartesian dualism seemed to emphasize the importance of certainty achieved through doubts as the basis of knowledge. Consideration of the coexistence of mind (thinking) and matter (biology) was acknowledged, but also that the mind in some ways could be distinct from the brain. One can have questions, false information, shaky interpretations, or other inconsistencies of the mind that are plausibly mental states, but not solely physical ones.

Mind-body research shows we think, anticipate, choose, execute, and essentially mindfully control our bodies and our lives. Anatomy is not necessarily destiny. Life experiences, including thoughts, can cause structural and functional changes in the brain. According to Elliot Valenstine in his 1998 book "Blaming the Brain," genes are responsible for establishing the fundamental organization of the Brain, but a large percentage of neuronal growth that leads to the establishment of potentially billions of connections has been shown to be influenced (if not guided) by experience. He stated genes do not produce behavior or mental states. Genes carry the instructions and templates for producing and assembling amino acids and proteins in the anatomical structures and experiences, remembered experiences from the past, present, and anticipation of future experiences. The expression of genes can also be turned off by physiological concomitants of life experiences.

Some popular theorists of ADD/ADHD behavior believe everything starts at the molecular level and remains a unidirectional process. Some molecular biologists maintain DNA is not so immutable, that genetic material undergoes a modification throughout the life span and at the cellular level of biological analysis there is a feed-back loop wherein the mind and the body can impact each other into a different course of action. It is a reductionist viewpoint that considers primarily studying only genes, neurotransmitters, cells, or organs. These structures may not allow an understanding of consciousness of thought, or the psychosocial context that shapes thought as well as these structures.

Somewhere closer to the heart of the debate about the nature of ADD/ADHD behavior in children must lie the question, "Is ADD/ADHD curable?" Some who hold tight to neurobiological explanations clearly state it isn't. It is considered to be either a life long disease or disorder, chemical imbalance, immutable temperament, or genetic and neurophysiological deficit. For others, to whom parenting is of primary importance, where in the scientific and professional literature is there sufficient data depicting cured children?

Webster's medical dictionary defines cure as "to make or become healthy, sound or normal again." Assume for the sake of furthering discussion that normal, or healthy, is defined as the absence of problems delineated in the DSM diagnosis. Perhaps a starting point would be to define cure as an inability to accurately diagnose a child as ADD/ADHD, in essence, a child who is "non-ADD/ADHD."

There seems to be a known and perhaps inescapable truth that clinicians and researchers must contend with. That truth being the observation that all one, two, and some three year old children act ADD/ADHD. Consistent with research on child development, and our understanding of cognitive and emotional growth in children, are observations that they tend to be active, curious, sensation seeking, distractible, egocentric, and in such apparent need of learning. A few years later, when in school or daycare settings, some children still act this way, at unacceptable times or places, and their behavior becomes much more of a clinical concern.

Where do we stand on the question of our psychological responsibility to view parents as teachers, their children as capable students of learning, and are matters of sustained attention and concentration, self control and reflectivity, or calmness in behavior acquired skills? Is it that some children are less capable of learning these skills because of genetically inferior or biochemically defective neurophysiological processes?

A second known and inescapable truth is that all children, whether diagnosed ADD/ADHD or not, seem to exhibit these behaviors in situation or stimulus specific manners. This may lead clinicians into an obsessional quandary as to how much is too much, with factors of frequency or intensity of ADD/ADHD behavior becoming the defining characteristic, rather than it's mere existence. What have we to say about the ability of a child to respond in a non-ADD manner if interested, motivated through contingencies of punishment or reward, or is seemingly under the hypnotic effects of a video screen. Couldn't it be that we have simply not understood and manipulated effectively, the environmental contingencies which motivate ADD/ADHD behavior change?

Consider a child brought to a clinician's office who obtains C's, D's, or F's in school. Stimulants were taken for some number of years. Various forms of mental health treatment occurred. Parents and teachers agreed on behavioral or emotional problems and perhaps learning disabilities. Concomitant problems of perhaps depression, anxiety, or Oppositional Defiant Disorder exist. The child scores in the ADD/ADHD range on various psychological tests requiring sustained attention, concentration, and reflectivity. These problems have existed for many years, at least prior to age six. Any reasonably minded individual could observe the child acting ADD/ADHD in multiple settings. Most would probably agree this child would be officially diagnosed ADD/ADHD.

What if this child's parents viewed ADD/ADHD as curable? They went to a clinician's office and engaged in regular, weekly, family psychotherapy, studying intensively the parent-child interactions and discussing parenting skills while the unconscious (unknown) elements which cause ADD/ADHD behavior were identified. What then would be said about the child if at termination and post-treatment follow-up the child moved out of special education and into mainstream classes, received A's and B's with no grades of C or lower, was medication free, scored non-ADD on psychological tests, was rated non-ADD on behavior rating scales by all teacher and parents, received teacher comments on report cards like "A pleasure to have in class," no longer had any coexisting psychological problems that were in existence at the beginning of treatment, and any adult could observe the child in any context such as home, church, restaurant, or school as "non-ADD/ADHD?"

It has been interesting to track the parents who did not follow-up consistently with my treatment to obtain information about their children along the same criteria. Follow-up interviews with parents who did not follow through with treatment recommendations typically included responses from a parent such as "Oh, my child is doing better." Then when the parent was queried on specific criteria for cure, most, if not all the ADD/ADHD criteria continued to exist in their child. Some of these parents kept their children on psychotropics, some relied on the school to solve the problem, some had their children in individual counseling experiences of short term duration, but none of these children and parents were engaged in a process designed to cure the behavior problem rather than "manage it" or "adjust or adapt to it." Unfortunately, it is these children that many researchers and practitioners seem to be writing about when they describe children as incurable.

This book is my attempt to share what I have learned during eighteen years as a clinical child psychologist and researcher—that ADD is a psychological (non-medical) problem and there is a drug-free, common-sense approach to curing ADD behavior. Children really do change and can learn to be better behaved. But in order to make this possible, parents must also change and learn to teach their children to be better behaved, or non-ADD. This approach is not easy. In fact, it may be the most difficult thing parents will ever do. It may also be the most important thing parents will ever do for their children and for themselves. This book, then, is an attempt to empower and motivate parents to take personal responsibility for themselves and for their children, and through psychotherapy to learn more about themselves and the reasons that their children misbehave. This book is also an attempt to challenge my colleagues and other related professionals to take another, much closer look at what we as mental health professionals are doing to help parents solve their children's behavioral problems.

The first chapters of this book describe the controversies and barriers to curing ADD children. Later chapters discuss the therapy or curative process. Ultimately, the book relays the personal experiences of parents who, through psychotherapy, learned how to produce a better behaved child. The book also contains case studies of children who came to me after years of behavioral and academic problems often treated ineffectively with drugs, who through psychotherapy were cured of ADD by anyone's definition.

I challenge readers to think about my opinions and practices. Compare mine with others' opinions on the causes and effects of ADD, and form your own educated opinions. Do not simply adopt anyone's ideas fully. Rather create your own theory of ADD and practice what is most honest and helpful for your child in your family.

1

ADD is Not a Medical Disorder or Disease

Men are disturbed not by things, but by the view which they take of them.

—Epictetus
(circa A.D. 55 - 135)

The dogma that "mental diseases are diseases of the brain" is a hangover from the materialism of the 1870s. It has become a prejudice which hinders all progress, with nothing to justify it.

—Carl G. Jung
(1916)

Where in the scientific literature are the one or few articles that constitute proof that ADHD is an actual disease with a confirmatory physical, or chemical abnormality? . . . As a neurologist making "disease" vs. "no disease" determinations daily, I have discovered and described real diseases, but found no disease in children labeled ADHD—no abnormality.

—Fred Baughman, Jr.,
Pediatric Neurologist
(1999)

Attention deficit disorder is a psychological behavioral problem "diagnosed" in the fields of psychology and psychiatry that is often referred to as ADD or ADHD. There is no medical or physical test or procedure to assess ADD. No blood test, head CT scan, MRI scan, EEG, physical examination, genetic test, or psychological test can diagnose ADD because ADD is a nonmedically defined behavioral problem. Diagnosis is based solely on a written list of behavioral criteria in the *Diagnostic and*

Statistical Manual of Mental Disorders. To be diagnosed as ADD, a child must be observed acting too impulsively, inattentively, and/or hyperactively for a period of at least six months, starting before the age of six. In addition, the child must display the inattentive, impulsive, or hyperactive behavior at times when it would be more appropriate for the child to act more calmly and with more attention and reflectivity in their thinking and behavior. According to this definition of ADD, most adults could easily be diagnosed with the disorder. In addition, all one-, two-, and three-year-old children are, by this definition, ADD.

The broad scope of the current definition of ADD, coupled with the inability to medically assess it, has led to ambiguity surrounding the diagnosis of the disorder. At the same time, controversy rages over what causes ADD. Medical explanations for ADD, such as genetic predetermination or biochemical disturbance in brain processing, dominate in the media, as well as professional, and nonprofessional opinions. In fact, it is the current trend to describe all psychological problems as "genetic" or "biochemical disturbances," including depression, anxiety, phobias, and drug or alcohol addiction. Substances called *neurotransmitters* are believed by some to be the cause of psychological problems; but no one can see them or measure them and then link these neurotransmitters to ADD behavior or to any other psychological problem with any credible scientific proof. Others have researched EEG tracings, brain tissue differences as shown on CT or MRI scans, and glucose metabolism changes as shown on PET scans as possible causes of ADD. Again, nothing conclusive has been found.

Some believe genetics is the cause but researchers can't completely separate out effects of genetics from the environment. The strength of environmental factors can have an effect on even the most obvious genetically predetermined features of our being. One could change the color of their hair or their skin should they so desire. Most genetic researchers admit that at best only fifty percent of the variance of behavior in individuals can be accounted for through genetic influence.

Genetic researchers typically study identical twins reared in the same family or separate families, and compare effects on various measures to fraternal twins reared together or apart or with non-twins reared together or apart. One problem in genetic research is that the environments of identical twins aren't necessarily always the same as the environments of fraternal or non-twin siblings. But some researchers assume "equal environments" even though there is some research evidence that parents treat identical twins more alike than fraternal or non-twin siblings and even that identical twins who grew up in different environments may have been treated more similar than fraternal twins in the same home. (Harris 1999) Some have shown the brains of "identical" twins may differ in structure. (Suddath 1990)

Genetic researcher Jay Joseph, in a recent article entitled "Not in Their Genes: A Critical Review of the Genetics of Attention Deficit Hyperactivity Disorder," (Joseph 2000) examines this "equal environments" assumption in genetic research and summarizes; "After an examination of the total weight of evidence in favor of a genetic basis or predisposition for ADHD, it is concluded that a roll for genetic factors is not supported and that future research should be directed toward psychosocial causes."

A critical reply to the Joseph article by two leading genetic researchers who purport a biological basis for ADD (Faraone and Biederman, 2000) disagree. However, in an earlier paper analyzing the issue of genetic versus environmental effects on ADD/ADHD, Faraone (1996) stated the following: "Although the genome is often viewed as a blue print for development, this metaphor does little justice to the dynamic interplay among genes and between genes and environments during development. Genes are switched on and off through the life cycle to meet the requirements of the developing organism. Given that the brain is developing through childhood and adolescence, it makes good sense to consider the possibility that the relative contributions of genes and environment to attention problems might fluctuate during development." Faraone stated in the same article, "At the outset, one common misinterpretation of genetic research should be avoided; the notion that all genetic disorders run an inexorable course that is resistant to change by therapies that do not address their genetic ideology . . . this attitude (of) 'therapeutic nihilism' is patently false."

Ruff and Rothbart (1996) in their book, *Attention in Early Development*, describe how attention and other cognitive skills develop in the first five years of life. They state, "Both neurological maturation and developmental changes in behavior occur in a social context. The newborn infant's regulation of state, the older infant's preference for novelty, and the preschooler's more voluntary attention all result from an interplay of the child and older, more experienced inhabitants of the child's social world. This interplay is possible, in part, because the child can share attention with others, an ability that develops in the first two years of life." They go on to describe how higher level attention and self control emerges toward the end of the first year, becoming more dominant and the development of this intentional system is dependent on social input. They state, "Higher level controls would not develop fully without the child's interaction with older, more experienced members of society. The young child depends on parents and siblings for help regulating state, for information about what is important to attend to and for guidance in how to meet social and cognitive demands. Parents and siblings, in turn, transmit values of the larger culture; their behavior directs the child to objects and events worthy of attention and demonstrates appropriate techniques of attending to everyday events and tasks."

Many mental health professionals have written with dismay about the trend in modern psychiatry toward "bioreductionism," the idea that every human trait can be traced to a specific gene. In a *New York Times* article, theoretical biologist Richard Goodwin states, "This genocentric view of biology is both misleading and dangerous because it engenders simplistic thinking, which prompts social acceptance of genetic determinism and turns personal responsibility into genetic destiny." (Blakeslee 1997). Harvard biology professors Ruth Hubbard and Elijah Wald (1993) observe, "The myth of the all-powerful gene is based on flawed science that has many dangers, as it can lead to genetic discrimination and hazardous medical manipulations."

In the April 21, 1997 issue of *U.S. News and World Report*, journalist Wray Herbert reviewed the evidence for genetic factors in everything from personality differences and homosexuality to alcoholism, mental disorders, and criminality. He summarized the multiple failed claims for genes that affect behavior. He concluded: "If there is a refrain among geneticists working today, it is this: The harder we work to demonstrate the power of heredity, the harder it is to escape the potency of experience. Yes, the way to intervene in human lives and improve them, to ameliorate mental illness, addictions and criminal behavior, is to enrich impoverished environments, to improve conditions in the family and society."

Professor Emeritus of Psychology and Neuroscience Elliot Valenstein (1998) states "A reductionist approach that studies only the properties of organs, neurotransmitters, cells, or atoms cannot understand consciousness and thought. Mental activity emerges from the integrated action of more than 20 billion brain cells (some of which are influenced by as many as ten thousand synaptic connections). Moreover, it is impossible to understand consciousness and thought without considering the psychosocial context that not only shapes the content of thought, but also the physical structure of the brain. Mental activity (normal or disordered) simply does not exist at a molecular level."

Nowhere is this more true than in the area of ADD diagnosis and treatment. A review of research conducted on ADD in the last thirty years reveals no conclusive evidence of genetic or biochemical causes of the problem. (Baughman 1996 and 1997; Breggin 1998; Cantwell 1996; Chowdhupry and Chattopadbyay 1995; DEA 1996; DeGranpre 1999; Diller 1998; Hooper and Tramontana 1997; McGuiness 1989; NIH 1998; Perry 1998.) In fact, there is at least equal *evidence* of psychological causes as there is for medical causes. Nevertheless, proponents of the disease/damage models of genetic or brain damage theories will cite many studies that they believe support their theories.

A recent review of empirical (scientific) evidence for the validity of neurobiological (brain damage) models of ADHD (Schulz et al. 2000) concluded that "inconsistencies in the literature do not allow unqualified support of any unitary model of ADHD." Neuropsychological evidence indicates that ADHD does not appear to be associated with deficits in sustained attention (despite the name), but rather, deficits in executive functions. But even tests of executive function have yielded inconsistent results. " . . . The precise nature of these deficits and their specificity to ADHD are clearly not resolved. Neuroimaging indicates structural and functional abnormalities of the PFC and basal ganglia; however this data must be considered preliminary for several reasons, including numerous discrepancies and the literature on the neurochemistry of ADHD is 'replete with inconsistent findings.'" The author stated molecular genetics has found some high risk alleles of several DA genes, but many children with ADHD did not have the high risk alleles. All in all, the author noted, "the precise nature of the pathophysiology has remained elusive."

The 1999 edition of the *Textbook of Psychiatry* (Hales and Yudofsky 1999) states that:

> 1. There remains considerable uncertainty about the validity of ADHD as a diagnostic entity. (p. 827)
> 2. Therapeutic responsiveness to a drug cannot be taken as a biological marker of a single disorder. (p. 827)
> 3. With unclear diagnostic boundaries, it is difficult to define or even conceptualize a unitary concept of ADHD or of its etiology. One generally cannot even specify the sequence of mechanisms involved, because biological findings that might play a role in the etiology might reflect effects of ADHD (p. 838)

A recent report on ADHD by the American Academy of Pediatrics (AAP 2000) confirms there is no known biological basis for ADHD.

Richard J. DeGrandpre, author of *Ritalin Nation: Rapid-Fire Culture and the Transformation of the Human Consciousness*, wrote a paper that appeared in *The Sciences*, March/April 1999. He described a recent study conducted at Stanford University (Vaidya et al. 1998). Investigators observed nineteen boys and classified the boys' behavior as ADHD or non-ADHD. Investigators then compared the MRI scans of the ADHD children with the non-ADHD children and believed they found that brain abnormalities existed in some of the ADHD children. Proponents of the study claimed that the findings could be useful in developing what they called "biologically valid criteria" for ADD diagnosis. DeGrandpre stated:

> The Stanford report garnered immediate attention because it held out hope for an end to the diagnostic frustrations, and it was hailed by the media as the discovery of a test that could readily identify ADHD. A typical headline appeared over

> the Associated Press story that ran in *The Boston Globe*: "Test Found to Identify Disorder."
>
> The authors of the study helped fuel the headline's assertion. In the Associated Press article, the psychologist John D.E. Gabrieli, one of the lead investigators, is quoted as saying the test gives a "brain signature" that specifically and biologically identifies people with ADHD. Similarly, a *Newsweek* headline announced: "Brain Scans Give New Hope for Diagnosing ADHD."

DeGranpre stated unfortunately, the public, and therefore the news media, are hungry for news of a sensational breakthrough in the field of human behavior. And all too often flashy headlines tout the latest study claiming genetic or chemical proof for the causes of human behavior or emotional problems. That is exactly what happened in the case of the Stanford study. No legitimate researcher would consider the results of this study proof of anything. Three of the non-ADD children were given brain scans, but were later dropped from data analysis for unreported reasons. This fact alone affects the credibility of the study. But that is not the only problem with this research, for the data that remained were far from conclusive. According to the MRI scans, two of the ten boys who were diagnosed with ADHD did not fit the MRI criteria for ADHD. Three of the nine boys not diagnosed with ADHD did fit the MRI criteria for ADHD. Either the original behavioral diagnoses misclassified five out of the nineteen boys, or the MRI data failed to provide "biologically valid criteria." The investigators concluded that the behavioral observations were reliable. In addition, the ADD children who participated in the study had been taking Ritalin for one to three years prior to the study, and dosage amounts varied among the subjects. It is impossible to know whether differences in brain activity in ADD subjects were the result of genetic/biological factors or simply the effects of long-term drug use. Further, for unexplained reasons, the children in the study were paid for their participation. The non-ADD diagnosed children received twice as much as the ADD children received for the same level of participation. Opponents of a psychological cause keep referring to the "large scientific literature" of studies purported to show a medical cause.

But see for yourself. Pick any study cited by individuals who believe in the medical cause for ADD/ADHD and read it closely to determine whether there appears to be any proof in it. Then, if you think it provides proof, try to find another study using the same method, and similar samples of children to see if it has been replicated. "There are none," you say? Truthfulness in science and our day to day lives dictates repetition must occur if we are to generalize causes of behavior beyond one individual or one study.

Ross and Pam (1995) state,

> Lately, it seems that not a day passes without the media proclaiming yet another sensational breakthrough in the search for the physical origins of mental illness. But beyond all the fanfare and media hype, is there a single shred of hard, empirical evidence to substantiate the existence of "a gene for alcoholism," or "the brain chemistry behind schizophrenia"? More to the point, in fact, is it scientifically sound to limit the search for the roots of mental illness to processes occurring within the body, while dismissing socioeconomic, familial, and experiential influences as, at best, mere "triggering mechanisms"? And, if not, what harm is being done by psychiatry's current obsession with these somatic chimeras?

Many researchers, and books shown to parents, still reference the previously famous Zametkin Study (Zametkin et al. 1990), which includes pictures of so-called ADD brains, even after the study has long since been discredited scientifically and never replicated. Numerous studies of children's brain scans since then are reported glowingly in major newspapers each year, still with no proof of a brain disease or disorder.

This type of research fuels much of the erroneous thinking about ADD. The distinction between what *causes* ADD and what brain differences are *correlated with* ADD is an important one. Even if the Zametkin study had resulted in conclusive findings, and even if the study could then be replicated, it would still prove nothing about causes of ADD behavior. The study would simply show that the brains of children labeled ADD will show different blood flow patterns while trying to solve a problem than the blood flow patterns in non-ADD behaving children solving the same problem. The study would not, however, address whether the ADD behavior was caused by a biological disease, or whether it was learned through ineffective parenting and education or other environmental events.

The Stanford study and others like it get researchers no closer to the answer to the age-old question of nature or nurture. Yet the biomedical model continues to dominate ADD research, and funding institutions such as the National Institute of Mental Health (NIMH) continue to focus on nature. Funding institutions show a marked failure to encourage research on the role of nurture—the developmental and societal origins of ADD. Nevertheless, the research into nonbiological origins that does exist does not favor a biological model. One example is the longitudinal research of Carlson et al. (1995). This study tracked several dozen children from birth through middle childhood and found that in "early childhood, quality of caregiving more powerfully predicted distractibility, an early precursor of hyperactivity, than did early biological or temperamental factors." Marital status at the time of the child's birth, level of emotional support received by the caregiver(s), and caregiving style were the most powerful predictors of later problems with distractibility and hyperactivity.

One can assume that behavior is multidetermined such that there are changes in brain biochemistry related to every human thought, feeling, or act. The issue is what came first and has primacy of control over the behavior in question. A curative approach with ADD/ADHD behaving children does not take a theoretical position that reduces the quality of the child's relationship with his or her parents to mere epiphenomena of the child's brain.

There is a tendency to translate all mental or subjective phenomena like thoughts, feelings, wishes, or beliefs into neurobiological events, but this denies existence of the potential idiosyncratic meanings of how a child's life came to be and does not allow clinicians to understand how specific behavioral deficits came about in a specific field. It minimizes the role of the mental functions of perception, choice, and learning. It does not help to teach parents about their child and allow for a fuller explanation of a parent's ability to understand and provide better functioning in the world at large.

To view ADD/ADHD as a symptom and perhaps a child's best adaptation to a complex set of conscious and unconscious factors within a family, such as contingencies of reinforcement and punishment, products of parental defense mechanisms, or imperfect or ineffective parenting allows a clinician access to make sense of the observed fact that children behave quite differently depending on the situation or circumstance.

A recent test revision of the DSM IV (APA, 2000) acknowledges the following, "it is very unusual for an individual to display the same level of dysfunction in all settings or within the same settings at all times. Symptoms typically worsen in situations that require sustained attention or mental effort or that lack intrinsic appeal or novelty (e.g. listening to classroom teachers, doing classroom assignments, listening to or reading lengthy materials, or working on monotonous, repetitive tasks). Signs of the disorder may be minimal or absent when the person is receiving frequent rewards for appropriate behavior, is under close supervision, is in a novel setting, is engaged in especially interesting activities, or is in a one-to-one situation (e.g. the clinician's office)."

The fact that ADD/ADHD behavior is "minimal or absent" under the aforementioned contexts implies the behavior may be more psychological than biological. This considerable variability in ADD/ADHD behavior amongst children has been a monkey on the back of geneticists and tempermentalists who are then left with the position of having to construct quite abstract theories of why children can act non-ADD in a variety of settings or under different stimulus controls.

The nurture theory, and the evidence that supports it in the fields of child development and psychology, is not as attractive or popular as the medical theory. This is partially because the creation of the scientifically nonvalidated belief that a child with ADD has defective genes or neurotransmission absolves parents, doctors, and society as a whole of the social responsibility to create healthier children. It is relatively easy to "link" ADD with heredity when an ADD child's parents and grandparents are also ADD. It is far more controversial to conclude that the child's relatives have taught their descendants to be ADD. Proponents of a medical theory fuel the flames of this controversy. One well-known advocate for genetic causes stated, "The hereditary nature of

ADHD now is a 'fact in the bag.' It would be a waste of time to regress 40 years to the heyday of psychoanalytic thinking when all childhood problems were attributed to bad parents—a not-so-subtle form of parent-bashing that lays the blame for ADHD and other complex developmental and mental disorders at the feet of the child's parents, family, and school. This is outdated psychoanalytical thinking, discarded decades ago by the scientific community for its explanatory uselessness, not to mention its cruelty toward parents seeking help for their children." Another went so far as to state that "nothing can cure ADHD." (Shaya et al. 1999).

To the contrary, using psychoanalysis to treat ADD is not cruel, nor is it useless. There are many who report the effectiveness of other psychological techniques or therapy approaches for the treatment of ADD. (Baldwin 1999; Kendall and Braswell 1993; Rosemond 1993; Stein 1999). Even Barkley, the outspoken opponent of psychoanalytical thinking who is quoted above, has unearthed evidence that supports the belief that nurture plays a primary role in the development of ADD in children. "Granted, family, school, and social environments can make the disorder worse. A large body of research, including my own studies, demonstrates that the way parents and teachers react to the behaviors of children with ADHD can exacerbate or diminish their severity and even contribute to other possible secondary problems such as frequent interpersonal conflicts with parents or teachers, low self-esteem, loss of interest in schoolwork, or even a drift toward delinquency." (Barkley 1995, 1998).

Psychoanalytic/psychodynamic therapies were essentially designed to study the psychological nature of parent/child interactions. The purpose of these "talking therapies" or "talking cures" is to elucidate the problems inherent in parent/child interactions in the most intense, in-depth, accurate, and honest way possible. By examining parent/child relationships in detail, these therapies give parents access to the answers they seek regarding their relationship with their children. Psychoanalytic therapy and talk therapy are not designed to "make things up" about parent/child relationships, but rather to discover and understand what takes place within these relationships more accurately and honestly. These therapies are not geared toward bashing parents, but toward enabling parents to take more responsibility for their lives and the lives of their children. Most talk therapists believe that parents and children can change, whereas those who condemn therapy boldly opine that parents and children with ADD cannot be cured. It is far crueler to tell parents that their children are incurable and must be medicated indefinitely than it is to provide parents with the answers that have been found by many talk therapists.

In addition to provoking relatively little controversy, the biomedical theory of ADD provides a much simpler solution—drugs. At first glance, drugging children with ADD seems like the perfect solution. Parents, doctors, and others are emphatic about the various "positive" changes drugs have produced in ADD children. Frustrated, upset, and anxious parents are quick to accept drugs as the easiest way out of an unbearable situation. However, under closer scrutiny, it becomes clear that the positive effects of the drugs are at most short-lived. Drugs are not cures when a child's life is examined in more detail. Drugs do not teach children completely appropriate behaviors that are needed throughout the course of a life. Drugs simply corroborate the helplessness and insecurity that ADD sufferers already feel—when they are told they cannot help themselves because they were made this way. Equally alarming is the fact that most, if not all, of the teenagers involved in a major teen shooting episode in the past few years were already on some type of psychotropic medication (Breggin 1999b, 2000a).

According to the recent National Consensus Conference on the Diagnosis and Treatment of Attention Deficit-Hyperactivity Disorder sponsored by the National Institutes of Heath, "After years of clinical research and experience with ADHD, our knowledge about the cause or causes of ADHD remain largely speculative. Consequently, we have no documented strategies for the prevention of ADHD." (NIH 1998). However, we continue to blindly treat behavior disordered children with drugs for fear that "[w]ithout this medication, such children will often experience the harsh moral judgment, censure, punishment, and social rejection reserved for those society deems lazy, unmotivated, selfish, thoughtless, immature and willfully irresponsible." (Barkley, 1995). I would hope that when someone else, including professionals, see me doing things that would cause ADD behavior in my children, they had the sense and fortitude to "bash" (correct) me if that's what it takes. Sometimes my wife has to "bash" me before it sinks in when I've been "lazy, unmotivated, selfish, thoughtless, immature, and willfully irresponsible," and she's not a scientist.

This book describes an alternative. The following chapters provide clinical proof that ADD is a psychological (non-medical) problem with a drug-free solution. Parents, not drugs, can and should set the stage and shape the possibility for their children's future psychological well being. Psychotherapy is a common-sense alternative to drugging our nation's children that can cure today's ADD epidemic.

2

Medical Treatment for a Psychological Problem

There's either a strange plague of hyperactivity in the U.S., or we've got a lot of folks prescribing Ritalin as a psychopharmacological nanny.

—Arthur Caplan,
Director, Center for Bioethics,
University of Pennsylvania

Sufficient data on safety and efficacy of long-term use of Ritalin in children are not yet available . . . Long-term effects of Ritalin in children have not been well established.

—Novartis Pharmaceuticals,
manufacturer of Ritalin (1998)

The view that ADD children are genetically dysfunctional, less evolved, or neurologically defective has probably done much more to impair a child's self-esteem and a parent's self-respect than holding children and their parents accountable to learn to "cure" this psychologically caused behavior problem. These beliefs stifle any search for a cure, and parents are left with the realization they and their child are incapable of change. An astute researcher, when actually looking at the sparse genetic research studies performed that supposedly support ADD being inherited, may be surprised to find that no conclusive evidence exists. Furthermore, the *methodological* weaknesses in these studies are numerous. Genes and DNA are never tested and linked to ADD behavior. In the few genetic studies conducted and those most frequently cited as "proof," the authors themselves state their research is inconclusive (Goodman and Stevenson 1989; Gjone et al. 1996).

CHADD (Children and Adults with Attention Deficit/Hyperactivity Disorder), the largest national parent support group, is quite biopsychiatrically oriented. The group receives considerable drug company financial support and professional advice from scientists and practitioners with biomedical viewpoints. One of their brochures states, "ADD is a neurobiological disability that interferes with a person's ability to sustain attention or focus on a task and to delay impulsive behavior . . . These brain metabolism studies, combined with other data including family history studies and drug response studies, have convinced researchers that ADD is a neurobiological disease and not caused by a chaotic home environment . . . Dealing with parental guilt—No, it's not your fault. Frustrated, upset, and anxious parents do not cause their children to have ADD. On the contrary, ADD children usually cause their parents to be frustrated, upset, and anxious." Many people believe this approach creates the impression in unsuspecting parents that their unfortunate child has been the recipient of "bad" genes. It is almost as if there is something floating around in the air we breathe, in the water we drink, in the brains inside our heads, in the neurotransmitters inside our brains, or perhaps in the DNA in the nucleus of our cells. However, ADD behavior is clearly visible. We commonly see ADD behavior in parent-child relationships.

Equally alarming were statements at the White House Conference on Mental Health in June 1999 when a keynote speaker said, "It is hard to believe that until twenty years ago we still believed that inadequate parenting and bad childhood traumas were the cause of psychiatric illness in children. And in fact, even though we know better today, that antiquated way of thinking is still out there, so people who wouldn't dream of blaming parents for other types of disease, like for child diabetes or asthma, still embrace the notion that somehow absent fathers, working mothers, overpermissive parents are the cause of psychiatric illness in children . . . and the only way we can change that is through more public awareness. I mean, essentially, these are no-fault brain disorders. These diseases are physiological, they respond to medicine" (cited in Breggin 1999b and 2000a). These statements that *parenting* effects do not have primary *influence* on a child's ADD behaviors are in contradiction with studies in the child development literature that show early parent-child (or caregiver-child) interaction patterns are more closely associated with causing ADD than temperament or biological factors (Carlson et al. 1995; Olson et al. 1990; Haddad and Garralda, 1992).

Parents *can* set the stage for and shape the possibility of future psychological problems in their children. Whether children will suffer in the future from depression, anxiety, drug problems, and even violence should legitimately concern parents. Society and psychologists often make parents irresponsible and abdicate their own professional responsibility for shaping America's mental health. When we do not support, teach, and hold parents responsible for their children's behavior we encounter serious trouble. One recommendation made by the keynote speaker at this above-mentioned White House conference is that society needs to evaluate and drug children even more. What participants failed to discuss at this conference was that in every major violent teen-shooting episode publicized in the last few years, most if not all of the teenagers were already on some type of psychotropic medication (Breggin 1999b). Evidence available to the general public so far reveals that not one of the teenagers' families had ever been to any kind of ongoing family or parent counseling to teach parents how *not* to raise violent children, or at least to consider psychological causes rather than biochemical or even sociological causes.

Estimates range from between 5 to 10 percent of the U.S. population of children are prescribed Ritalin and/or diagnosed ADD, according to various sources (Hoagwood et al. 2000). This number seems to be rising every year, and many medically-oriented thinkers contend we are not prescribing enough drugs to children. One state survey in 1995 of nearly four hundred teachers found that 40 percent of elementary school and 32 percent of junior high school students were diagnosed ADHD and medicated with psychostimulants, most commonly Ritalin (66 percent) (Runnheim, 1996). Another study shows that of children placed on psychostimulants 80 to 90 percent are boys (Zachary, 1997). Furthermore, a recent 1999 *American Journal of Public Health* article (LeFever et al. 1999) describes a survey conducted in a Virginia school district on about 30,000 students. Seventeen percent of white boys and 7 percent of white girls were medicated for ADHD, and 9 percent of African-American boys and 3 percent of African American girls were medicated for ADHD.

The International Narcotics Control Board (INCB) has been concerned about the use of Ritalin and has monitored this problem since the early 1990s. A more recent INCB annual report (1999) indicated that treatment rates for ADD in some American schools are as high as 30 to 40 percent of a class. Concern was raised that North Americans are particularly interested in taking performance-enhancing drugs, and this drug use may be linked to culture and lifestyle more than in other countries of the world, although in Canada, Ritalin prescriptions have risen to two or three times as much in the last few years.

Using prescriptions for amphetamines in the long-term to solve behavioral problems in children and adults remains problematic in other ways. A 1995 United States Drug Enforcement Administration report (DEA, 1995) on methylphenidate (Ritalin) found that it was among the top ten most frequently stolen controlled pharmaceuticals. Students are selling their medications to classmates who are snorting the powder in the same way one might snort cocaine. A DEA report cites a 1994 high school survey indicated more seniors in the United States abusing Ritalin than the amount of the drug legitimately prescribed. Diverse segments of the population, from health care professions to children and junkies, abuse Ritalin. Randomly selected hospital records of ER admissions for drug use effects rose from 271 in 1990 to 1,044 in 1992. Ritalin can be addictive. No conclusive studies exist regarding its long-term effects on individuals. Furthermore, production of the drug has increased six-fold since 1990. In fact, the U.S. manufactures five times more Ritalin than the rest of the world combined.

A recent article in the *Archives of Pediatrics and Adolescent Medicine* (Rappley et al. 1999) presents a study of Michigan's state-sponsored Medicaid health care program data on 223 children aged three and under whom doctors diagnosed with ADD. Of those 223 children, 57 percent were taking drugs for this problem, while only 27 percent were being treated through sessions with a psychologist. For ADD toddlers, doctors prescribed 22 different drugs in 30 combinations. A third of the toddlers were taking two or three drugs simultaneously.

An article in the 1998 *Journal of the American Academy of Child and Adolescent Psychiatry* (Zarin et al. 1998) reports that 97 percent of children with ADD who see a psychiatrist, as opposed to a psychologist or some other type of mental health practitioner, end up on drugs. Forty-nine percent end up on two or more drugs. Most recently (Zito et al. 2000) a *Journal of the American Medical Association* article entitled "Trends in the Prescribing of Psychotropic Medications to Preschoolers" found 12.3 percent of children ages two through four in two state Medicaid programs were prescribed stimulant drugs. There was a three-fold increase in prescriptions from 1991 to 1995. A related article expresses concern over the fact that there were 3,000 prescriptions for Prozac written for children less than one year old in 1994 (Grinfeld, 1998). A follow-up Harris Poll the day after the Rappley et al. study appeared asked the question: "Do doctors overprescribe drugs like Ritalin and Prozac for children?" Seventy-six percent of the respondents (11,658 voters) answered *yes*; 8 percent (1,337) voters answered *no*; and fourteen percent (2,277 voters) answered *don't know*.

Many mental health practitioners excuse misbehavior in children by essentially stating that the propensity to misbehave is genetic or at least brain-mediated. So they actively advocate increased drugging of children. "If children are born to misbehave, why make parents suffer longer than necessary? Let's identify children and drug them earlier." More children and teenagers now take psychotropic drugs, yet more delinquency exists today than in the past. Some biologically-oriented mental health practitioners argue that we simply had not *seen* the ADD problem or had not identified misbehavior as well as we could have in the past. Obviously, people who make this argument have not actually worked in the schools or in the juvenile justice system over the last thirty years and are not aware that there were *fewer* ADD-behaving kids in the past.

A rather interesting political development occurred when the Colorado State School Board voted six to one on November 11, 1999 to pass a resolution warning of the possible negative effects of psychotropic (mind-altering) prescription drugs on school children. The state of Texas has recently followed suit. This resolution came to pass for many reasons: parents feeling pressured by educators to put their children on Ritalin, the increasing public awareness about overmedicating children, school funding for children labeled "learning disabled," a possible connection between prescription drugs and violent behaviors in children, and concerns about misdiagnosing children. The Colorado resolution stated: "Whereas the Colorado State Board of Education recognizes that there is much concern regarding the issue of appropriate and thorough diagnosis and medication and their impact on student achievement; and, whereas there are documented incidences of highly negative consequences in which psychiatric prescription drugs have been utilized for which are essentially problems of discipline which may be related to lack of academic success . . . be it further resolved that the Colorado State Board of Education encourage greater communication and education among parents, educators, and medical professionals about the effects of psychotropic drugs on student achievement and our ability to provide a safe and civil learning environment" (Johnson 2000). An Internet opinion poll through the *Rocky Mountain News* polled respondents, asking the question, "Was the State Board of Education right to attack the use of Ritalin?" Eight hundred and ninety respondents (96 percent) said *yes*, and 41 (4 percent) of respondents said *no*. (Education Reporter 1999)

In a major report from the British Psychological Society (Reason 1999), British physicians and psychologists are warned not to follow the Canadian and U.S. practice of applying the label attention-deficit/hyperactivity disorder (ADHD) to such a wide variety of behaviors in children. Above all, the report urges restraint when prescribing psychostimulants: "It must not be the first, and definitely not the only, line of treatment." The report by the society working party is based on the literature, information, and advice from a variety of organizations and professionals in Canada, the U.S., Europe, and Australia. According to the report, "The idea that children who don't attend or don't sit still in school have a mental disorder is not entertained by most British clinicians." It is estimated that some 90 percent of those identified as having ADHD in the U.S. are prescribed stimulants at some time during treatment.

Americans are overwhelmingly the biggest users of prescription psychotropic drugs compared to any other country in the world. In a 2000 paper by Richard J. DeGrandpre in the journal *Cerebrum*, the author points out that with the exception of Canada, the profile of stimulant use outside the U.S. looks dramatically different. More Ritalin is consumed in the U.S. than the rest of the world combined, and use in North America accounts for about 96 percent of the world's Ritalin consumption. While stimulant drug use in the U.K. increased as much as fifty-fold in the 1990s, per capita use remains ten to thirty times less than in the U.S. The U.K. is among a number of countries identified by the International Narcotics Control Board of the United Nations as showing a troubling increase in childhood use of stimulant drugs. Spain also shows rapid growth, whereas medium growth has occurred in

Australia and Israel, with little or no growth in countries such as France and Germany. In France, a country of 57 million people, about 100,000 Ritalin pills were dispensed in 1998, whereas in Canada, a country of 31 million people, 56.5 million pills were dispensed that same year. Differences in stimulant use correspond to the number of diagnoses of ADHD, which is essentially unheard of in France, where family structure is more intact and child development is still viewed as a psychosocial rather than as a biomedical issue. If Americans consume more than 90 percent of the world's Ritalin, should we believe the arguments that, "Well, we consume a lot more of everything else in the world, too" or "It's because we are more scientifically advanced or ahead of everyone else"? Maybe, but why is it that in China, Japan, Europe, France, Germany, and England, they do not use nearly as much medication? Are American children better behaved? Are they healthier? Do they perform better in school? Are they more industrious? Or does it have more to do with different lifestyles, family structures, or our medical and cultural beliefs/values?

3
Drugs for ADD

. . . Many people stumble through life to the very edge of the abyss without knowing where they are going. At times, this happens because those whose vocation it is to give cultural expression to their thinking no longer look to the truth, preferring quick success to the toil of patient inquiry into what makes life worth living.

—Pope John Paul II

Once ADD behavior is considered a problem, that is, behavior that one would desire to change, then the next step is to figure out how to change it. Many believe that prescribing stimulant medication or amphetamine-like substances such as Ritalin, Adderal or Dexedrine is the most helpful treatment approach. Some justify this treatment based on a belief of a medical cause, and some justify this treatment based on simply using the medication to modify, suppress, sedate, or numb behavior, which drugs can sometimes do. While Ritalin can effect behavioral change in some children, this does not give evidence of a biochemical cause. Many chemical substances and drugs can suppress or control human behavior. Author David Stein (1999) writes:

> Even if well conducted research were to reveal physiological differences, it would still not mean the presence of a disease. Such differences could not only be the result of environment but also from long periods of being on Ritalin, or related drugs, or even the result of the constant, self-induced state of agitation ADHD children keep themselves in. If these differences were truly ever found, they'd have to be very subtle because we're having so much trouble finding them. And even then these differences would probably be within the normal

range for kids that merely have more active levels of behavior and not a disease.

Children with ADHD are assumed to have a biochemical abnormality because Ritalin produces a "paradoxical" slowing of activity and increases attention span in these children. Studies by Judith Rapoport (1978, 1980) and her colleagues at the National Institute of Mental Health, however, demonstrated that the response of ADHD children to amphetamine is not paradoxical at all. These investigators administered Ritalin to children of professionals in the biomedical and mental health community and found that the drug also decreased activity and increased attention span in these *normal* children.

I suppose the answer to whether drugs work depends on your definition of "work" and the intentions of the drug seeker. To some, drugs seem like a wonder pill. To others, whatever the short-term benefit, clinical research reveals very little, if any, long-term benefits. To many, the harmful effects clearly outweigh any potential short-term benefits.

It has been my experience that all children have side effects from these drugs, although they sometimes don't report them. Parent and doctors don't *see* these effects of blood pressure changes, heart palpitation, or brain chemical changes, so they don't pay as much attention to them. If adults took as much as is prescribed for their children, a comparable adult dose for body weight, there would be much more complaining and fewer prescriptions written. Children have complained to me that they don't like how it makes them feel, especially when they get to the preteenage years. Adults I know who've taken them by prescription or to experiment tell me they don't like how it makes them feel either.

Children are often not given medication when they are out of school, such as during vacations and weekends. I have found that this is not because the child does not misbehave or is never required to pay attention outside school; rather, parents do not feel accountable to teachers or principals for this misbehavior. More importantly, parents feel ambivalent about medicating their child. As one mother put it, "He's mine on the weekends. I don't want him on that stuff." Another mother said, referring to changes in her child after having been put on Ritalin, "He wasn't my Tommy. His imagination was gone." A *Wall Street Journal* (McGuinnis 1997) article quoted a mother describing her son on Ritalin, "I missed him. He wasn't there. He did everything he was supposed to do, but his personality was gone."

Frequently, parents seek help after medication has been tried but has failed to create a long-lasting improvement. McGuinness (1989) theorizes that a drug regime provides a brief respite for parents for up to one year, during which time a physiological tolerance occurs, and then the child's acting-out behavior slowly returns.

There is a price to pay for drugging children. For researchers and clinicians to minimize their negative effects and state that drugs are "safe" because children have not yet grown three ears as an obvious side effect is insensitive and inconsistent with what we know about them.

The *Physicians Desk Reference* (PDR 1998) is the standard encyclopedia used by physicians, which lists all of the prescription drugs manufactured in America. According to the PDR, "Ritalin is a mild central nervous system stimulant. The mode of action in man is not completely understood, but Ritalin presumably activates the brain stem arousal system and cortex to produce its stimulant effect. There is neither specific evidence which clearly establishes the mechanism whereby Ritalin produces its mental and behavioral effects in children, nor conclusive evidence regarding how these effects relate to the condition of the central nervous system." With regard to ADD it states, "Specific etiology of this syndrome is unknown, and there is no single diagnostic test. . . . Sufficient data on safety and efficacy of long-term use of Ritalin in children are not yet available." Over twenty potential side effects from its use are described in detail. Ritalin is not a normally or naturally occurring substance produced by the human body, so it will produce side effects simply because one is taking amphetamine-like substances regularly. Similar wording is listed for the other commonly prescribed drugs Adderall and Dexedrine.

Ritalin is a Schedule II controlled substance with many of the same pharmacological effects as amphetamine, methamphetamine, and cocaine. Using Ritalin can produce a number of similar effects familiar to those taking speed, such as increased heart rate, changes in respiration and body temperature, appetite suppression, and increased alertness. Common side effects of weight loss or growth retardation have been considered potential side effects of chronic use. In its published pamphlet entitled,

"Prescription Information," the manufacturer Novartis (1997) reveals numerous potential side effects such as "nervousness, insomnia, loss of appetite, abdominal pain . . . lower seizure threshold . . . some patients taking higher doses may not grow up as fast as other children. Their growth rate very often 'catches up' once the drug is stopped. . . . chronic abuse can lead to marked tolerance and psychic dependence." The pamphlet's authors make it a point to state that abuse would occur if Ritalin is taken too much or at higher doses, yet also state "long term effects of Ritalin have not been well established." The questions parents need to ask is, safe or not, are there *healthier* alternatives to Ritalin?

The publication of the American Psychiatric Association, *Treatment of Psychiatric Disorders* (APA 1989), observes that cocaine, amphetamines, and methylphenidate (Ritalin) are neuropharmacologically alike." As evidence, the textbook points out that abuse patterns are the same for the three drugs; that people cannot tell their clinical effects apart in laboratory tests; and that they can substitute for each other and cause similar behavior in addicted animals. The *Diagnostic and Statistical Manual of Mental Disorders* by the American Psychiatric Association (1994) confirms these observations by placing cocaine, amphetamine, and methylphenidate abuse and addiction into one category.

An editorial comment in the *Archives of General Psychiatry* (1995) states, "Cocaine, one of the most reinforcing and addictive of abuse drugs, has pharmacological action very similar to those of MPH (methylphenidate), one of the most commonly prescribed psychotropic medications for children in the United States." The remarks were inspired by a report in the same issue of the journal by a group led by N.D. Volkow (1995). Using the PET scan, the researchers found that the distribution of cocaine and methylphenidate in the brain is identical, but that Ritalin remains for a longer period of time.

More recently Volkow and colleagues (1997) observed: "Methylphenidate (Ritalin), like cocaine, increases synaptic dopamine by inhibiting dopamine re-uptake, it has equivalent reinforcing effects to those of cocaine, and its intravenous administration induces a 'high' similar to that of cocaine." Volkow and her team have shown that oral Ritalin consumption dramatically increases dopamine availability—even at therapeutic doses—though the increase takes place over a much slower time period than when Ritalin is delivered intravenously. In another article (1999) Volkow wrote that she found it interesting that these researchers wanting to study cocaine's effects on the brain chose to use methylphenidate (presumably because it would be illegal and unethical to give research subjects cocaine). They note that "methylphenidate has pharmacological properties similar to those of cocaine," and "when it is injected intravenously, cocaine abusers report that it has effects similar to those of intravenous cocaine." Indeed the subjects of this study reported cocaine craving induced by methylphenidate. If Ritalin is administered "in sufficiently large doses, at high enough frequency, and over a long enough period of time," have children taking Ritalin become drug addicts? As Volkow's research shows, though some children may not experience a drug "high," they nonetheless experience a chronic pharmacological assault on the brain similar to the one experienced by regular cocaine users. Clinically, older children, adolescents, and especially adults do sometimes report a "high" and a stimulant effect, which at least partially explains its abuse potential and illegal street sales in high schools and colleges. When researchers describe new studies they believe may finally identify the medical basis for ADD, such as "dopamine transporter systems" (reviewed in Journal Watch Psychiatry, 1999) they may simply be measuring the chemical alterations of Ritalin use.

Genetic researchers have focused lately on whether something called a dopamine 4 receptor gene (DRD4) or a dopamine transporter gene (DAT1) are related to ADD/ADHD behavior. A recent review of the "Genetics of Childhood Psychiatric Disorders" (State et al. 2000) covering the last ten years of the literature on ADD/ADHD revealed various researchers have been unable to replicate findings of previous studies and in spite of "the intense interest among the scientific community as well as the lay press and general public" there has been nothing conclusive found.

The authors make the following assertion at the end of their review:

> It may be that for some child psychiatric disorders, vulnerability genes of relatively small effect will be identified and the individual genetic background and early environmental experiences will be found to be far more salient than the effect of any single gene. In this case, it is likely that

> interest in genetic issues per se will recede and that other models of pathogenesis will emphasize the importance of the multiple other factors influencing brain and behavior. All told, since it will be easier in the foreseeable future to change environment and behavior rather than to change genes, the ability to allow researchers to tease out environmental determinants could well be the most significant clinical contribution that geneticists will make over the next decade . . . Many of the genes identified may likely be 'susceptibility' and not 'causative' genes.

Stimulant drugs may reduce some aspects of ADD behavior in children through their effects. Swanson and colleagues (1993) reviewed the "cognitive toxicity" caused by drugging children. They stated, "In some disruptive children, drug-induced compliant behavior may be accompanied by isolated, withdrawn, and overfocused behavior. Some medicated children may seem 'zombie-like' and high doses which make ADHD children more 'somber,' 'quiet,' and 'still' may produce social isolation by increasing 'time spent alone' and decreasing 'time spent in positive interaction' on the playground."

Arnold and Jensen (1995) also comment on the "zombie" effect caused by stimulants. They state, "The amphetamine look, a pinched, somber expression, is harmless in itself but worrisome to parents who can be reassured. If it becomes too serious, a different stimulant may be more tolerable." These behavioral responses in children to drugs are often considered "improvements or desirable effects in those who seek to impose greater control over their children's ADD behavior."

When parents discuss medicating their child, pediatricians will often describe problems such as headache, stomach ache, and loss of appetite; but sometimes they may give a parent a mistaken impression that these drugs will produce non-ADD behavior. By non-ADD behavior, I am referring to the capacity to pay attention, concentrate, act calmly, and, most importantly, become interested and curious about learning, listening, and reflecting. In essence, while drugs may decrease ADD behaviors, they do not increase or develop non-ADD behaviors that parents seek in their children such as getting better grades in school or getting along with others.

Drugging children does not teach creativity, calmness, reflectivity, or attention; it just suppresses the undesirable opposites of these behaviors. Non-ADD behaviors have to be taught and learned in relationships with others such as parents or teachers. When a child is medicated, one must ask the question, is the drug-induced symptom alleviation seen as positively therapeutic or helpful, or simply the toxic effect of the drug?

In a comprehensive literature review on the pharmacological effects of stimulants, psychiatrist and author Peter Breggin (1998) writes:

> Millions of children in North America are diagnosed with Attention-Deficit/Hyperactivity Disorder and treated with psychostimulants such as methylphenidate, dextroamphetamine, and methamphetamine. These drugs produce a continuum of central nervous system toxicity that begins with increased energy, hyperalertness, and overfocusing on rote activities. It progresses toward obsessive/compulsive or perseverative activities, insomnia, agitation, hypomania, mania, and sometimes seizures. They also commonly result in apathy, social withdrawal, emotional depression, and docility. Psychostimulants also cause physical withdrawal, including rebound and dependence. They inhibit growth, and produce various cerebral dysfunctions, some of which can become irreversible. The "therapeutic" effects of stimulants are a direct expression of their toxicity. Animal and human research indicates that these drugs often suppress spontaneous and social behaviors while promoting obsessive/compulsive behaviors. These adverse drug effects make the psychostimulants seemingly useful for controlling the behavior of children, especially in highly structured environments that do not attend to their genuine needs.

What is called "spontaneous" behavior, including exploration and novelty-seeking, is at the heart of normal functioning for animals and humans. Any animal—including monkeys, rats, mice, or pigeons—has a natural curiosity or tendency to explore its environment. Ritalin and other stimulant drugs suppress this whole range of behavior—the spontaneous, exploratory, investigative, playful, and social activities of animals . . . as well as children.

In a recent literature review entitled "Empirical, Ethical, and Political Perspectives on the Use of Methylphenidate (MPH) Ritalin" (McCubbin and Cohen 1999), the authors state:

> Reliance upon a psychoactive medication to make children "ready to learn" is not only unsupported by the evidence, it teaches children incorrect lessons about how to meet the stresses and challenges of life. . . . Meanwhile, it is doubtful whether MPH's negligible effects on certain short-term cognitive tasks in experimental studies provide the major impetus to the use of MPH, given the greater prescription of the drug for hyperactivity. Methylphenidate's suppressive impact on disruptive conduct easily explains why schools are eager to promote MPH for "problem" children, particularly as class sizes increase, corporal punishment is banned, suspensions and failed grades are less favored, teachers get saddled with managing various social problems such as illicit drug use, suicide, or sexually transmitted diseases, and psychosocial professionals and helpers in the schools become scarce. In sum, at least in the short run, MPH subdues disruptive behaviors such as restlessness, exploration, acting out, and aggressiveness. Teachers often see the control of such behavior with MPH as aligned with their interests. If such effects were not achieved in the short run, continued recourse to MPH would likely have faded by now.

Higher-level learned behaviors, strategies and coping skills continue to develop throughout childhood and adolescence, but these are clearly far too complex to be "ameliorated" by a drug impacting directly on the brain. Hence, if Ritalin were to have a basic and lasting impact upon problem behaviors via neurological processes, it would have to be administered while the child is still a baby. However, there is absolutely no reason to suppose that the use of stimulants or, indeed, of any psychotropic ingested by children while developing their most basic skills and personality while their cerebral structure is quite malleable would have any positive long-term effects. There is every reason to believe that such use would powerfully impair normal development.

It is therefore distressing to note that the use of Ritalin in the United States is growing fastest among preschoolers. Perry's review of brain development (1998) indicates that early life experience shapes the neuronal connections and organization of the brain. Current research in neuroscience reveals the brain regions most relevant to developing higher cognition, including reasoning and problem solving, self-regulation, and personality, have a maturational course extending into adolescence. (Thompson and Nelson, 2001) The use of Ritalin in young children could alter normal adaptive processes in the brain and replace them with pharmacologically-induced changes. Ultimately, the stimulant could become an integral part of the functioning of the child's psychology.

Perhaps the most common critique of the use of Ritalin is that it is used to treat part of the range of normal behavior or even behavior that should be valued rather than repressed. Children are highly curious and exploratory, easily bored, and physically much more active than adults. Play and spontaneous movement are crucial elements of childhood development.

Physical activity is simply an expression of the energy of youngsters or a question of learning to use one's body. Such activity provides glucose to the brain and enables increasing nerve connections, making it easier for children of all ages to learn (Hancock 1996). Young children indeed require more synapses than adults. Later brain development partly proceeds by selecting, in interaction with the environment, which synapses will be favored and which will wither away.

As many of us know from the experience of "cramming," drugs can temporarily enhance focus or attention. Their use, however, does little to further the elements of true higher-level learning. This includes comprehension, the ability to connect knowledge with other learning, and the ability to apply what is learned to new situations (generalization).

The argument that Ritalin improves learning should therefore be turned on its head. Childhood offers a variety of developmental opportunities that we fail to exploit when, instead, we provide a limited semblance of learning through the administration of Ritalin. Rather, we need to encourage education geared to maximize children's potential by working with their natural curiosity and activity (rather than suppressing them). Further, children may learn the wrong lessons by being given Ritalin, including the mistaken belief that education is something to be absorbed passively, instead of being actively discovered. Whalen and Henker (1997) state in their review:

> Stimulant pharmacotherapy is often construed as an aid to help children and families negotiate rough spots and potholes in the developmental terrain, or as a means of modulating arousal and self-control so that children with ADHD can benefit, like their peers, from everyday opportunities to acquire cognitive skills and adaptive coping strategies. But if stimulants actually facilitate skill acquisition, wouldn't one expect the gains to maintain after treatment ends? One of the most nettle-some enigmas surrounding stimulant pharmacotherapy is the difficulty of documenting long-term advantage despite reliable evidence of short-term gain. It is often disheartening to observe how rapidly behavior deteriorates when medication is discontinued. Apparently, whether a child is medicated for 5 days, 5 months, or 5 years, many problems return the day after the last pill is taken.

One issue, discussed earlier, is that the gains are often temporary and may not enhance long-term adjustment. A second issue concerns the degree of improvement and questions about whether behavior and performance are actually "normalized." Often the changes appear to be both desirable and meaningful but insufficient, and the likelihood of normalization remains an open question.

A third issue concerns the problem domains that respond to treatment. Children with ADHD are multiproblem youngsters, often experiencing not only the core symptoms of ADHD such as disinhibition and disorganization, but also many related difficulties such as academic failure, peer rejection, and low self-efficacy. In most instances, the problems exist for several years before treatment begins, and thus by the time a child comes to professional attention he or she may already show delays or deficits in several areas of functioning. After beginning stimulant pharmacotherapy, the child may now be able to listen to the teacher, focus on the task at hand, and complete one task before beginning another; but she may not have mastered the fundamental reading or mathematics skills needed to complete assignments at her grade level, and she may lag far behind her peers in her capacity to organize task components, plan successive problem-solving stages, and monitor her own progress. The child may now talk rather than shout, request rather than grab, and wait his turn when playing a game with peers; but he may not know how to initiate a conversation, join an ongoing group activity, or provide social support to a friend. A child's mother and father may now be able to tolerate and even enjoy their child, but they may not know how to set age-appropriate goals, gauge the optimal level of challenge, provide reasonable incentives and consequences, and deal with the inevitable mishaps or relapses in ways that promote growth and family harmony.

We know that pills don't teach skills, that stimulants may lead to improvements in only some performance realms, and that there are broad individual differences in medication responsiveness. Thus it is more the rule than the exception that adjunctive interventions focused on academic skills, peer relations, or parenting competence will also be needed. In their review article, Fisher and Greenberg (1997) state the following:

> We would urge caution with respect to the sometimes enthusiastic position that Whalen and Henker (1997) adopt about stimulant treatment for ADHD. This highlights again the subjectivity and the ultimate uncertainty that prevails in arriving at decisions about any of the psychotropic drug treatments. One can perhaps best illustrate the uncertainty that exists by comparing the Whalen and Henker viewpoint with that of McGuiness (1989) after she completed an extensive review of the pertinent literature concerned with the use of

> stimulant drugs for ADHD children. McGuiness said simply: "The data consistently fail to support any benefits from stimulant medication" (p.183). Interestingly in a 1991 review, Whalen and Henker seemed to be closer to the McGuiness stance: "Despite the impressive track record established by stimulant therapies over the past two decades, this treatment has serious limitations. Not all children can be given these medications, nor do all who take them improve. In the majority who appear to benefit, the changes may be short-lived or may persist only as long as the drug regimen continues.

McGuiness (1989) concluded that 25 years of research had failed to "pin down a disorder that does not exist" and that "drugs do not work. They help the teachers and parents, but they do nothing for the children. Other studies reveal there is little if any long term benefit in academic achievement or cognitive functioning (Gadow, 1985; Jacobvitz et al., 1990)

Kohn (1989) questioning why Ritalin is used in the first place, suggested that the drug "may have much greater relevance for stress reduction in care givers than intrinsic value to the child."

Swanson et al. (1993) in their literature review emphasized the limitations that have important implications for educators. This point-of-view review suggested that (a) stimulant medication may be overused in the United States; (b) the short length of action critically limits the benefits of typical treatment with stimulants; (c) the high doses may produce cognitive toxicity; (d) many children with ADD have adverse responses to stimulants; (e) in most cases, stimulant treatment is stopped within two years; and (f) treatment with medication has no residual effects that continue after the pharmacological effects dissipate.

According to repeated studies by the United States Drug Enforcement Administration, production of Ritalin has increased six-fold since 1990. The U.S. manufactures five times more than the rest of the world combined. Beyond the results of DEA reports, it is estimated that about one third of the U.S. population has used some form of medication in an attempt to improve their psychological or behavioral functioning. This does not count those who use alcohol or cigarettes. If we are concerned about the "drug problem in America," we need to look more closely at the source of our need for drugs. Namely, why do we spend so much effort at medicating ourselves rather than on other arguably more effective methods of achieving better psychological functioning that are already available to us?

4

Money—In Research and Practice

I do not suggest that either they [the drug companies] or we [the American Psychiatric Association] are evil folks. But I continue to believe that accepting such money is, in the long run, inimical to our independent functioning. We have evolved a somewhat casual and quite cordial relationship with the drug houses, taking their money readily. . . .

We seem to discount available data that drug advertising promotes irrational prescribing practices. We seem to think that we as psychiatrists are immune from the kinds of unconscious emotional bias in favor of those who are overtly friendly toward us. . . . We persist in ignoring an inherent conflict of interest.

—Fred Gottlieb,
APA Speaker of the House
(1985)

The past 25 years has led to a phenomenon almost unique in medical history. Methodologically rigorous research indicates that ADHD and hyperactivity as "syndromes" simply do not exist. We have invented a disease, given it medical sanction, and must now disown it. The major question is how we go about destroying the monster we have created. It is not easy to do this and to save face, another reason why physicians and many researchers with years of funding and an academic reputation to protect are reluctant to believe the data.

—Diane McGuinness
Professor of Psychiatry
(1989)

It is difficult to get a man to understand something when his salary depends upon his not understanding it.
—Upton Sinclair
(1878-1968)

Scientific and clinical practices are affected by the social values of their time and place. Significant influences affecting the search for medical causes can involve the tremendous amounts of money given to physicians, self-help organizations, and other public information sources from pharmaceutical companies. Pharmaceutical companies spend billions of dollars in advertising and research geared toward the sale of prescription medication. I'm unaware of any studies funded by these companies to look into psychological causes with psychotherapeutic treatments through family therapy approaches. In a recent article in the journal *Academic Psychiatry* (Christensen and Tueth 1998), researchers made the following pronouncements after collecting data on drug companies: "Pharmaceutical companies mean business. In the United States alone, pharmaceutical manufacturers spend in excess of $10 billion dollars per year on promotion and advertising. In 1988 they spent an estimated $5,000 per physician, and in 1993 this amount swelled to more than $13,000." A *Washington Post* article states, "*Fortune Magazine* rates pharmaceuticals as the nation's most profitable industry. No. 1 in return on revenues (18.50%), assets (16.6%), and equity (39.40%)."

National Public Radio reported recently that the Center for Responsive Politics reviewed data from official disclosure reports by lobbyists and found that, "the five industries with the biggest lobbying budgets are insurance, pharmaceuticals . . . ranked #1 and #2 respectively."

An article appearing in *The Journal of the American Medical Association* entitled "Physicians and the Pharmaceutical Industry: Is a Gift Ever Just a Gift?" contains a meta-analysis of 29 studies, which indicates that physicians are very influenced by drug companies. Drug companies spend $8,000–$13,000 per physician on things such as gifts, meals, honoraria, and travel. Doctors usually deny that drug companies influence their prescribing practices, but there is a strong measurable relationship between receiving a gift or meal from a drug representative and prescribing a drug or requesting a formulary addition—even when the new drug has no advantage over older, less expensive drugs. Accepting an all-expense-paid trip from a drug company influenced prescribing practice up to two years later. Inaccurate information and some inappropriate treatment decisions were associated with lunch rounds with speakers representing pharmaceutical companies (Wazana, 2000).

Interesting social policy changes include ADD behavior now being considered a "disability" by our school systems as well as the Social Security Administration. There is potentially significant financial reinforcement for remaining "disabled" in our society, especially when being told ADD is out of our behavioral control. "Is there an ADD epidemic sweeping our nation about learning disabilities or is it about learning to be disabled? Is it about neurotransmitters and chemical imbalances or is it about increased market share for drug companies, increased funding for research, increased business for practitioners, increased funding for special education and disability, increased sales of books, tapes, seminars, and other products and services? Are children the raw materials of the ADD industry? Have children simply become funding mechanisms to be screened, labeled, and medicated?" These are the words of Sue Parry in her 1998 paper, "ADHD: A Market Based Affliction?" (Parry, 1998). Social influences teach our children that they should look toward a medical cause for their behavioral difficulty in life.

Disability status and some medical theories may tend to create a longer-term problem by giving parents the impression that life is more limiting than it has to be, whereas life is a potentially exciting, rewarding learning experience. Discussions with some parents, some school teachers, and some guidance counselors reveal many expectations by parents that it is the school's responsibility to teach a child to pay attention, concentrate, and act calmly. Payment for psychological treatment for ADD problems through insurance companies is on the decline. Prescription medication is preferred rather than the more costly longer-term psychotherapeutic approaches, especially in managed care programs. It is as if there is an unstated social movement toward decreasing responsibility of parents and families for the psychological development of their children.

Fred Baughman, a pediatric neurologist from El Cajon, California has written extensively on various issues related to the "ADD fraud" and has been quite active politically in trying to confront the conflicts and debates inherent in the misdiagnosis and treatment of ADD problems in children. Dr. Baughman has openly challenged misinformation in the ADD controversy, leading medical and disease model researchers into admitting statements that are much closer to the "scientific truth" about the so-called proof that ADD is caused by brain biochemistry or genetics. (Baughman 1997, 1999). Baughman states, "Over the past 30 years, psychiatry has denigrated and jettisoned the human willpower-coping model and psychotherapy. It claims instead that all character flaws and emotional pains are 'diseases,' the result of biochemical imbalances of the brain, to be 'balanced' with drugs. Were organized psychiatry not 'one' with the pharmaceutical industry with drugs to sell, the espousal of 'biopsychiatry' and of one-dimensional drugging for illusory diseases might be difficult to understand." In the past few months class action suits against drug manufacturers, the American Psychiatric Association, and others have been filed claiming the parties conspired to create a broad-based definition of hyperactivity disorders that had an effect on boosting profits. The drug manufacturers are also charged with utilizing false and misleading advertising, which played down the drug's side effects and oversold the drug's benefits.

As noted by Knapp (1997), "psychosocial therapies have no 'product champions' to fight in their corner." This is a clear disadvantage in a climate where decision makers reduce budgets. In contrast, enormous interest groups support the medicating of children, including the pharmaceutical industry, the educational/health establishments, organized biopsychiatry, and parent groups that seek to exert greater control over their children. In the United States, the Congress and government agencies also fund these powerful interest groups.

Many parents, doctors, and school teachers have realized that prescription of drugs do not "cure" ADD and that the ADD behavior problems never go away completely with drugs prescribed. The problem of ADD is often viewed as a life-long disorder, disease, or disability that will last a lifetime. Witness the recent interest in "Adult ADD.'" Imagine the profit motive in a disease that requires many years of "medication."

Clinical research takes a lot of time and costs a lot of money. There has always been discussion about the financial motives or influences of drug companies and how much the professions of psychiatry and psychology are economically driven. Sometime it's not money that drives research but beliefs in ideas that are designed to justify one's professional existence. There's a lot of research data that comes out on TV, and someone has to pay for those expensive TV ads. Information about curing ADD through psychotherapy and studying the psychological causes of ADD is not something that most people seem to want to pay for. An overwhelming majority of research studies on ADD are supported either directly by drug companies, and researchers at colleges and universities who seek grant money will tend to get rewarded more for "medical studies" rather than "social sciences research." Funding sources for research projects into child development, parenting, or family dynamics is abysmal. Someone has to pay for the research or the college professor/researcher's studies (salaries). Who does them for free?

An interesting letter to the editor by a Dr. Mandelkern (1999) appeared in the February 1999 *Journal of Clinical Psychiatry*:

> In reading the *Journal* over the past years, I have found that articles examining specific medications are frequently funded by the manufacturers of those medications, a fact accessible in the small print at the beginning of each article. I have wondered what sort of relationship might be found between support of research and favorable outcome. To examine this question, I reviewed all regular issues of the *Journal* for the year 1997, not including supplements, which are largely sponsored by pharmaceutical companies. I identified all articles that studied outcome or tolerability for a specific agent and separated them according to their support by the manufacturer or absence of such support, as listed at the front of the article. I then rated outcome in each article as favorable or unfavorable with respect to the manufacturer's drug.

The data from Dr. Mandelkern's study demonstrate that support by a manufacturer correlates with favorable outcome of the reported study. Conversely, lack of support makes it much more likely that the study will not reflect favorably on the use of the medication. In other words, it is more likely for pharmaceutically-sponsored trials to show data that are favorable to the drug studied than studies that are not supported by drug manufacturers.

The editor responds to Dr. Mandelkern:

> Rigorous clinical investigation tends to be expensive, which means that someone has to fund it. Much research in psychopharmacology is funded by the pharmaceutical industry, whose primary motivation is profit. . . . A separate question is whether positive results are more likely to be published than negative results. In psychiatry, as in all of medicine, the answer appears to be yes. Dr. Mandelkern's observations suggest that this is even more likely when a study is funded by a pharmaceutical manufacturer. I must note, however, that a pharmaceutical company goes to great pains to construct studies that are likely to turn out in its favor. There are instances, however, when academic investigators are pressured not to publish negative findings——phenomenon that has recently been publicized and properly condemned.

Not only are drug studies potentially biased, numerous flaws exist in the assumptions and methodology in the studies themselves. An excellent review and critique by Jacobs (1999) states, "The usual standards cannot produce a realistic picture of either safety or efficacy."

A recent edition of *Pediatric News* (Bates 1998), a trade paper received by many pediatricians, presented in bold print on the front page the following article entitled, "Medication Makes The Difference in ADHD Children - Psychosocial Therapy Made No Difference." The article reported a study that was promoted quite heavily to many people, not just pediatricians. It provides a good example of how research studies tend to perpetuate the belief in the importance of ADD behaviors being medicated. The article features a recent study sponsored by the National Institute of Mental Health (NIMH) entitled "The Multi-Modal Treatment Study for Attention Deficit Hyperactivity Disorder" (MTA Study)

(MTA Cooperative Group 1999), which was published December 1999 in the *Archives of General Psychiatry* after many months of positive publicity in the psychiatric and general media. Investigations at multiple sites were designed to assess four treatment conditions: (1) medication management alone, (2) combined medication management and behavioral therapy, (3) behavioral treatment, and (4) community care. The aim of the study was to "resolve controversies and clinical quandaries about the relative value of medication and behavioral treatments."

A critical examination of the MTA Study was conducted by Peter Breggin, M.D. at the International Center for the Study of Psychiatry and Psychology (ICSPP) (Breggin, 2000c). The findings were as follows: The MTA was not a placebo-controlled, double-blind clinical study. There were no placebo groups or control groups. The raters who were relied upon to provide effectiveness ratings of various treatments were not blind to the treatment. They knew which children were taking medication and which weren't. Rater and researcher bias, consciously and unconsciously, can heavily influence the outcome of these types of studies. The only blind raters (raters who did not know which kids were in which treatments) found no difference in any of the treatment groups i.e. behavioral interventions were equal to medication interventions. The blind raters observed children in the classroom only, and found no differences between drug and non-drug treatment groups.

In this study behavioral interventions were no better or worse than drug interventions. There was no nontreatment control group because two thirds of the community-treated group received a variety of medications as well as other interventions and could not be considered a nontreatment control group. Thirty-two percent of the medication management group was already on medication for ADD at the start of the study. Of 144 medicated kids, 46 were already on medication at the start, and the children selected were probably those who already responded positively to prior medication. The medication management group was highly selective. The study initially screened 4,541 children who were referred from a variety of sources. The aim was to draw a broad spectrum of children typically seen for ADD services, but of 4,541 children only 12 percent of the subjects (579) were selected. This means that the children in this study may not have been representative of children in the general community. The medication management group was relatively small. From a seemingly large scale study of 579 children who entered the trial, only 144 entered medication management and received medication alone. Thirteen of these children dropped out before starting, limiting the group to 131. Eight more dropped out during the study for a total of 123 finishers in the medication management group. So of the original 4,541 children screened, only 123 or 2.7 percent were actually in the medication management group.

The children did not rate themselves as improved on the tests they were given in any treatment category at any time. The children were apparently given a depression rating scale, but no data were reported on that depression rating scale. Stimulants can commonly cause depression in children, and this raised the question of whether the depression self-rating scales were dropped because they indicated a worsening of the child's condition. Boys represent a disproportionate number of children who are medicated with stimulants. One reason stimulants are used is to suppress behavior in boys, making them more controlled; and despite efforts to recruit more girls, 80 percent of the subjects were boys. It was not clear how a placebo washout was used. Subjects who responded to placebo were dropped from the study. This tends to skew studies to favor drug effects and disregards placebo effects.

Drug treatment was continuous for 14 months. Behavioral treatments were stopped earlier. Behavioral treatment was spaced out to one a month or stopped. The behavioral treatment used techniques developed by a psychologist who is very pro-drugs and pro-medical explanations for ADD. The behavioral treatments were not those used by many psychologists in private practice or by myself with the children studied in this book. The behavioral treatments used tended to view the child as a defective object suitable for control by parents and teachers rather than a child in conflict with adults at home or at school. This approach tends to ignore what is known about family systems therapy and the necessity of changing overall patterns of relationships within a family, starting with parents. It was not family therapy or parent counseling therapy. Nonetheless, these limited behavioral approaches did as well as all the other treatments, according to the only blind observers in this study.

Sixty-four percent of the children were reported to have adverse drug reactions (ADRs), 11 percent moderate and 3 percent severe. The kids' reactions tended to be dismissed because they were in the category of "depression, worrying, irritability," explained as possibly being due to "nonmedication factors." It is likely that these problems of depression, worry, and irritability were reactions to the medication. The adverse drug reactions were recorded on a two-page checklist by teachers and parents. There was no apparent training for the process. Parents and teachers were reassured in writing that the drug was safe and that ADRs were not serious, thus creating a bias. Furthermore, many ADRs such as behavioral suppression, loss of spontaneity, apathy, and increased obsessive behavior, are often seen as improvements by parents and teachers.

The authors admitted no improvement or difference in academic performance in spelling or math. The tables seem to indicate no improvement in reading as well. Overall, no academic improvement was found as the result of any treatment. There was very little effect on social skills. Social skill differences among the treatment groups were limited to a significant difference favoring combined treatment over "standard community care." Neither was better than behavioral or medication management treatments.

All the principle investigators are well-known drug advocates. The six principle investigators have devoted much of their professional life to encouraging the concept of ADD and drugging children. The parents and teachers were exposed to pro-drug views. Families and teachers were given materials before they enrolled in the study. The "Teacher Information" for the study presented the usual claims about how much harm ADD causes children, and it stated that the children would be treated with "a safe and effective dose of medication." That kind of built-in bias can certainly affect a study that uses teachers to rate safety and efficacy. The "Information for Parents" handout had similar built-in biases, including a reference to biochemical imbalances and genetic factors in ADD. There is even a question whether the parents in the study were given informed consent about risks posed to their children by drug use.

This study employed an "intent to treat" analysis. This method uses data from kids who dropped out of the study. For example, a kid who dropped out of the study because of adverse drug reactions could be counted as successful if on his or her last visit a positive evaluation was reported. The study has been highly promoted by advocates of drug therapy as a demonstration of stimulant treatment for ADD. In fact, the study failed to meet basic scientific criteria for a drug trial and empirical research. If anything, the study confirmed that medication treatment was no better than other treatment approaches for helping children diagnosed ADD. Too many factors invalidate the study. Very few valid conclusions could be drawn from it.

Most discerning is that the MTA Study failed to examine the kind of interventions that in actual clinical practice prove very effective in helping children diagnosed ADD. These interventions include individualized family counseling aimed at improving relationships in the family and individualized education approaches that inspire children to engage themselves in school. When parents of ADD-behaved children come for help in the real world, they are seeking assistance through therapy or counseling, not the so-called behavioral treatment or community care treatment presented in this study. The non-drug treatment conditions in this study were not the same kind of treatment I practice and describe in this book.

At this time I'm unaware of any research publications or books listing sufficient numbers of case studies of children who have actually gone through common psychotherapeutic experiences as did those children (and their parents) in my case studies. Very few full-time clinical practitioners with views similar to mine publish papers or research, or describe the therapy process, none very extensively on the subject of ADD behavior, often due to lack of time, money, or motivation.

5

ADD—Social and Cultural Cure

When the family is in order, all the social relationships of mankind will be in order.

—I Ching
(circa 12th century B.C.)

Johnny was not lazy, nor was the school failing to educate him decently: He had a learning disorder. Or he had an attention disorder. And the root of these disorders was a biological or neurological or genetic glitch. Poverty was let off the hook. Social injustices were let off the hook. Parents were let off the hook. Lousy schools and dysfunctional teachers were let off the hook. There was simply something biologically wrong with these children that accounted for all the things that teachers, parents, and Boy Scout leaders did not like about a whole panoply of childhood behaviors: not sitting still, not paying attention, not learning to read correctly (on time), butting in. . . .

—Louise Armstrong,
And They Call It Help (1995)

Even "good" psychopharmacology decreases the need to scrutinize the child's social environment and may permit a poor situation to continue or grow worse. Should dysfunctional family patterns and overcrowded classrooms be tolerated just because Ritalin improves the child's behavior? . . . Should society use a biological fix to address problems that have roots in social and environmental factors? If it consistently does, how might society be affected? . . . The rise in the use of stimulants is alarming and signals an urgent need for American society to reevaluate its priorities.

—Lawrence H. Diller,
pediatrician and author, *Running on Ritalin* (1998)

> *Psychotropic drugs have taken an increasingly prominent place in easing the pains of living in the late 20th century. This is partly due to the technological changes which have made these drugs widely available. Drugs are a seductive option to apparently "dealing with" poverty, alienation, oppression, abuse, perceived loss of "community" and sense of purpose, and the decline of our schools and family life. One danger of psychotropics is that their effects are felt in so many realms (organic, psychological, interpersonal, social, sociopolitical and economic). In this way, drugs alter current circumstances powerfully and distract us from other ways of explaining and resolving distress. Medawar (1998) wrote of the use of tranquilizers and antidepressants that ". . . the more people, individually are helped by such drugs, the greater the danger that those drugs will sustain and promote the very conditions that led to their use in the first place. If they work, [these drugs] do so by raising tolerance to stress. To this extent they enable society to accommodate more stress. The effect, in the end, is simply to let more stress in. The "disorder" called ADHD and its "treatment" epitomize this reflective dynamic between individual and social factors."*
>
> —Michael McCubbin and David Cohen (1999)

What is presented as "scientific knowledge" to parents about ADD is determined by differing philosophical views on the nature of human behavior. What is considered science is considerably dependent on prevailing social trends in attitudes and values. Differing views exist about how science is to be defined, and those who identify themselves as scientists or researchers also disagree on what is an appropriate or valid object of scientific inquiry. In other words, to understand what is truly scientific, one needs to trace the roots of philosophical views on the nature of human beings as well as current social and medical trends to understand the relevance of current or modern day scientific opinion about our children.

Many of our current social values and practices can be linked to what is important to the current scientific community of our times. What is popularly scientific is what is presented most often to the press through the news media and other written works. Current thinking and practices on ADD behavior in children can truly be considered influenced by what is currently politically and scientifically "correct." In a circular manner, what is important to modern day society influences and shapes scientific research and practice patterns. Understanding this will help parents understand some of the reasons why there is so much misinformation about ADD.

Earlier in human history, philosophy (or the study of ideas and the meaning of life) and science (the attempt to investigate the validity and workings of what is observed) went hand in hand. In 300 B.C. Aristotle studied astronomy and zoology as well as logic and ethics. There was an appreciation for what was physical and tangible as having an important relationship with ideas, thoughts, or essentially, mental processes.

As human scientific and philosophical understanding evolved, there has always been a question of how much is "nature" versus how much is "nurture." Nature is that which is typically more biological or in the physical realm of life, while nurture consists of all of life's experiences after birth that are not necessarily biological. Modern day medicine, put in an historical context, seems to favor cures for human suffering that are biologically based. Physicians and other healers of the past termed charlatans, barbers, or snake-oil vendors co-existed with those physicians who practiced bloodletting and lobotomies. Those who practiced from a less biologically-based orientation included witch doctors, shamans, and various "faith healers." But there has always been a tendency toward physical explanations and means of alleviating human suffering versus spiritual, sociological, or psychological methods. There were those as well who offered real relief from human suffering, such as priests and the clergy utilizing faith and spirituality or physicians utilizing medicinal substances and bodily manipulations. The tension among beliefs about what is most effective in relieving human suffering as emanating from something biological versus mental or spiritual continues to exist.

Toward the end of the sixteenth century, philosopher Frances Bacon, was considered the godfather of the "scientific revolution." He advocated generalizing from specific instances of observed phenomena to scientific laws or theories that could be tested by experiment. He held that both experience and reason were necessary to come to know the world.

Another philosopher, Rene´ Descartes, Bacon's contemporary, was often considered the founder of modern philosophy. Descartes gave us the famous distinction between mind and matter (Cartesian dualism). He emphasized the importance of certainty achieved through doubts as the basis of knowledge. He articulated the coexistence of the mind (thinking) and matter (biology). There was also an acknowledgment of the dichotomy between mind and body and that the mind could be distinct from the brain. One can have questions, doubts, false information, shaky interpretations, and inconsistencies in the mind; but the mind does not have illness unless it has an unidentifiable physical problem, in which case one should see their physical or medical doctors. Ideas and beliefs are plausibly mental states, but not solely or at all physical ones. We can think, anticipate, choose, plan, execute, and essentially mindfully control our bodies and our lives.

Descartes coined the famous phrase, "I think, therefore I am." This laid the conceptual groundwork for the importance of thought relative to the senses and emotion as the key to understanding. Unfortunately, psychiatry and especially neuroscience often falls into the trap of dualism of the mind and the body wherein the mind has no matter and the body has no mind.

Later philosophers, often considered empiricists, like the late 1600s British philosopher and physician John Locke, posed the idea of the mind of a newborn child as a *tabula rasa,* or blank slate. He believed our minds were completely impressionable and that all knowledge is impressed upon us from outside ourselves. He divided ideas acquired from experiencing into two types, sensations (or information we get through seeing and hearing) versus reflections, the information we get through introspection and processes of the mind like thinking, imagining, or believing. Beginning with a blank slate means that children can acquire values and prejudices long before they have the ability to form their own. Children can accept things uncritically. This has important implications for parents and anyone else responsible for molding young children's minds.

There are some who believe that reality consists only of material forces as described by physics and chemistry. This tends to be linked to scientific materialism, which claims "the mind itself is only the result of the workings of matter." This philosophy of materialism would seem to go hand in hand with our present-day materialism and emphasis on that which is not necessarily spiritual, psychological, or philosophical. There almost seems to be an inclination to avoid contemplating higher level explanations or purposes of pleasure, pain, sensation, gratification, or responses to immediate emotions or impulses as being under the control of thoughts. An excellent reference detailing the history of scientific and philosophical thought and how differing views of human nature evolved can be found by reading Lou Marinoff's book *Plato, Not Prozac* (Marinoff, 1999).

The belief that people are highly formed at birth but find a mentally different temperament or predisposition to advance in certain ways is an old idea. The Roman physician Galen, developing the idea of Hippocrates, proposed around 190 A.D. that it is neither the slaves nor the gods that determine what we want or what we do; rather, it is to the balance of our bodily fluids, the four "humours," as they were called. If our blood dominated, our temperament was "sanguine," or "eagerly optimistic"; if our black bile or gall dominated, then we were "melancholic" or "doleful in temperament." The choleric temperament was "passionate," and if phlegm dominated, then we were "phlegmatic" or "calm in temperament" (Marinoff 1999).

Plato was more interested in the individual's capitulation to the sacred order than in underlying temperament. He named the sanguine the "iconic" character, endowed with the artistic sense; the melancholic, the "pistic" character, endowed with the playing-caretaking role; the choleric, the "noetic" character, endowed with the intuitive sensibility, playing a moral role; the phlegmatic, the "dianoetic" or rational character, endowed with reasoning sensibility, playing the role of logical investigator in society (Marinoff 1999).

Scientists in the 19th and 20th centuries changed how we viewed the causes of behavior. Ivan Pavlov wrote about his famous experiences wherein animal behavior seemed more under the control of environmental events such as the sound of a bell associated with reward. Famous behaviorist B.F. Skinner wrote extensively about human learned behavior; he considered environmental rewards and punishments to be primary when considering causes of behavior. Pavlov and Skinner were "cutting edge" thinkers, whereas at this time in the literature, our physiology was still said to determine our attitudes and actions, not deities or heavenly bodies.

A third view concerning what causes human behavior is one which transcends biological and environmental theories, and that is a belief in God or spirituality. Religious beliefs do not necessarily undermine or replace the biological or environmental views, but can sometimes explain human behavior as a result of spiritual forces or something more transcendent. A continuing philosophical debate exists today over the concept of what is free will versus what is God's grace (doing). While the existence of free will is still debated, it is crucial that we view the human mind as having the capacity to at times be self-directing.

In the early 1900s Sigmund Freud, a neurologist and eventually a psychoanalyst, practiced in a time when almost everything in medicine was thought to be biologically oriented. In his earlier writings he believed that every "mental illness" was caused by a brain disease but eventually discarded that notion when he found the powers of suggestion, hypnosis, and free association could relieve an individual of mental and physical suffering. He was shunned by some in the medical community of his day for his "crazy ideas" about the unconscious and that the mind and psychological factors could affect someone's physical health.

Many years after Freud, American medicine, and the field of psychiatry in particular, focused more on mental or psychological cures to human suffering through the development of psychoanalytic treatment and talking therapy. Then in the 1950s and '60s, drugs or medicinal cures for suffering came back into increasing popularity again until the 1980s when what is often referred to as "the biological revolution in psychiatry" seemed to predominate in medicine. The 1990s were described by many in the field of medicine as "the decade of the brain." The term "brain" meant its neurotransmitters and physical structures rather than thoughts, beliefs, attitudes, and consciousness, also located in the brain.

Interest in the biological aspects of the brain has coincided with increased technological sophistication. We also live in a period when money and speed are highly valued in society. Current culture includes e-mail, computers, cellular car phones, satellite technology, fax machines, answering machines, VCRs, cable TV, the Internet, and video conferences. We are in a sense "wired and stimulated," speeded up day and night, constantly sending and receiving messages. Anything that slows that process down is viewed as too painful. Time is considered a premium. There are many social pressures on medicine to find something quick and easy to fix (DeGrandpre 1999).

While American research science seems to be in a current historical swing toward interest in the biological aspect of the mind, the medical profession and psychiatry have not found anything biological that definitely cures human emotional or mental suffering.

The medical profession of psychiatry and psychology has identified many syndromes, referred to as *disorders*, that have never been shown by any existing scientific criteria to be conclusively caused by anything biological or neurological. When something exists without scientific evidence to back it up, it is what philosophers call *reification*. Psychiatrists and psychologists are social experts at reifying syndromes and disorders and then making inferential leaps as to the causes. Indeed, "mental illness" is not a proven scientific phenomenon, but more of a metaphor for what at times can be mistaken for reality.

The terms *mental illness* or *disorder* still have medical connotations that often legitimizes continued prescription of "medical treatments" such as drugs, while no medically-based illness for any common psychological problems in life has been proven to exist. Much of psychiatry seems intent on proving the existence of psychological problems, and human suffering to be organic or biological, a brain or genetic disease. At times the search for psychological or nonmedical causes appears to be abandoned. Nevertheless, while the psychiatry profession has continued to search for mental illnesses, there have been those who criticized the profession, such as psychiatrist Thomas Szasz. In *The Myth of Mental Illness* Szasz states, "The notion of mental illness is used today chiefly to obscure and explain away problems in personal and social relationships, just as the notion of witchcraft was used for the same purpose from the early Middle Ages until well past the Renaissance" (Szasz 1961).

Dr. Sydney Walker III, a neurobiologist, psychiatrist, and author of *A Dose of Sanity*, says that the *Diagnostic and Statistical Manual of Mental Disorders* has "led to the unnecessary drugging of millions of Americans who could be diagnosed, treated, and cured without the use of toxic and potentially lethal medications." He later stated the following: "It is time for psychiatrists to return to being physicians—not seers, priests, gurus, or pill pushers, but real physicians. It's time for them to start asking what's really wrong with their 'hyperactive,' 'depressed,' and 'anxious' patients, and to start uncovering and treating the causes of their problems—not just hiding their symptoms under layers of dangerous and addictive drugs" (Walker, 1996).

Psychiatrist Peter Breggin, often referred to as "the conscience of American psychiatry," in his book *Toxic Psychiatry* (1991) describes how the current dominant ideology of a powerful medical and pharmaceutical establishment frequently announces "breakthroughs" in brain chemistry to justify its use of drugs, electroshock, and involuntary hospitalizations and other "treatments." The belief that the origins of psychological pain and suffering stem from biological factors continues to justify the use of electroconvulsive therapy (ECT), a literal electrocuting or shocking of an individual's brain in the belief that ECT is the most reasonable cure for someone's depression or unhappiness.

Candace Pert (1997) summed up while testifying on Capitol Hill, "I believe that the data clearly show that the mind is not confined to the brain, but impacts on every organ in the body. . . . One day we will look back regretfully on this strange mindless era of blatant overmedication and cavalier surgery for pain with psychological roots as we now regard the ignorant era of medicine in the 19th century when germ theory was unknown and physicians scoffed and persecuted those who thought washing the hands was important."

While there is a tendency to avoid psychological or philosophical explanations for the workings of the mind, society at the same time seems to pursue with considerable interest that which is tangible and responds primarily to our senses rather than our thoughts and sense of values and spirituality. Americans have a psychological weakness for the quick fix. We want drugs. We look to technology to improve our lives and provide easy answers and effortless comforts. We eagerly embrace excuses that reduce personal responsibility for anything we can't quickly or easily figure out or accept. Much easier to relieve ourselves of our burdens by considering our unhappiness and misbehavior a disease, something genetic or biological rather than environmental, and thus far beyond our control. We busy ourselves with technological advances, the accumulation of wealth, the pursuit of pleasure, and the search for solutions to diminish our pain. Much social and medical justification moves us toward a biopsychiatric accommodation to life. Rather than emphasizing the importance of one's mental life or mindful operations about a child's ADD behavior, which are quite observable and amenable to change, there is a continued search for the immediate relief of painful experiences caused by presumed biomedical phenomena.

Peter Breggin (1994, 1997) has described the fallacies of biological psychiatry and psychotropics in particular. He proposes the main effects of these biological interventions is to blunt the sensitivity of people to the conditions of life around them. If this blunting of sensitivity is taken to be the cure, then that lessens the opportunity to resort to a more perceptual or psychological means to deal with what is a perceptual or psychological problem. But this problem is massive because the belief in biological causes and cures for human suffering is what is most popular in current day medicine. Breggin states on the cover of his 1994 book *Toxic Psychiatry*, "Why therapy, empathy, and love must replace the drugs, electroshock, and biochemical theories of the 'new' psychiatry."

In his 1999 book *Ritalin Nation: Rapid-Fire Culture and the Transformation of Human Consciousness*, Richard DeGrandpre describes in a very convincing cultural analysis, from someone who has training in pharmacology and psychological sciences, the following view:

> Ritalin is a drug, a stimulant drug, used in the psychiatric treatment of millions of children in the United States. These children are said to suffer from attention deficit disorder (ADD), which Ritalin treats by calming them down. *Ritalin Nation* is the story of the fastest culture on earth—American culture—and how this culture of speed has transformed human consciousness and, in doing so, created a nation hooked on speed and the stimulant drugs that simulate speed's mind-altering effects. For most of us, our dependence on pharmacological versions of speed begin and end with caffeine. For millions of others, however, the pharmacological solution to the

> growing need for speed extends far beyond the occasional can of Coke or cup of coffee. These solutions include powerful stimulants like cocaine, methamphetamine, and Ritalin, all of which have very similar pharmacological properties.
>
> The "ADD" child is of course the perfect example of the need for constant sensory consumption. Studies have documented, for example, how hyperactive attention deficit children turn into everyday normal children under sensory-rich conditions. They have shown how these children begin to fall apart when the sensory stream begins to fade. They have also shown how, under suboptimal sensory conditions, children are calmed by the backdrop of stimulation that Ritalin so elegantly provides (a pharmacological effect that also happens to occur in most children). Thus, for the millions of children who are currently lining up for Ritalin, and for the many thousands of adults who have also begun to use it, the problem has less to do with an innate brain dysfunction, for which there still remains no scientific evidence, and more to do with how the rise of rapid-fire culture this century has transformed human consciousness.

Andrew Morrell (1998) in writing about narcissistic disorders in children states the following:

> The growing popularity of ADD as a diagnosis is a cultural phenomenon worth exploring as a function of narcissistic pathology. There is an obvious appeal to viewing one's child's (or one's own) life difficulties as a correctable, genetically determined, biochemically based disorder. It eases the feelings of guilt and responsibility that we as parents feel when our children fail to thrive, in school or elsewhere, and allows us to feel that we did the best we could in the face of circumstances beyond our control. In addition, it holds out the promise that, if only the right medication is found,

> we can regain the perfect child we dreamed of having—who could be, have, or do all we could not—in place of the child we actually have. It also assuages the fear that one's child is "fated" to suffer from the same flaws and limitations that the parent did. Finally, it offers the hope that all that is wrong within the family can be righted without the parents' being forced to reflect too much on how the family's established mode of interacting, or the emotional tenor of their relationships, has contributed to their child's being who they are.

Morrell approaches the problem of ADD from the perspective of narcissism. Narcissism is a psychological term usually implying preoccupation with one's own needs relative to another's in circumstances when another's needs should be given more attention and value. ADD-behaving children are too self-centered (narcissistic) in their behavior. There is often less focus on the needs of others such as teachers, parents, and peers. However, ADD-behaving children are observed to be non-ADD behaving when engaged in activities that seem uniquely interesting or important to them.

When parents and society abdicate responsibility for learning how to teach children to be less self-centered (ADD), they are allowing self-centered or ADD behavior to occur. As toddlers, children are normally self-centered, but beyond toddlerhood the behavior becomes a disorder or is termed "pathological." Hand in hand with the self-centered approach to life goes a blaming of others for one's unmet needs rather than developing a healthier adaptation and cooperation with others, whether it be by observing laws, rules, or the expectations of parents and teachers. The active pursuit of blaming a child's brain or DNA, coupled with a drug fix or cure, is in a sense social narcissism which feeds our needs for the quick fix materialistic pleasures, numbing of pain and discomfort, and abandoning of the search for psychological causes or personal responsibility.

If people could learn to live more with their fear of feelings and become more confident in their ability to tolerate pain and delay gratification, this would enable society and parents specifically to learn to teach their children these important skills. We easily forget that pain and suffering exists for the purpose of signaling there is a problem, as well as to motivate us to change. To prematurely focus on eliminating pain without awareness of its cause(s) would be like medicating an infant's crying because it is too irritating without knowing whether the child needs a diaper change, is hungry, or needs to be held. We often determine a child to be "colicky" without further investigation of possible psychological factors or perhaps even unforeseen and unmet physical needs. The emphasis must be on pursuing thoughts, dreams, and one's associations to life and connect these with our mind's ability to think and make choices rather than acting so much on impulse and one's sensory capacities. In other words, the painful feelings and behavior caused by children labeled ADD could be interpreted as a beneficial signal. Pain does not always have to be suppressed immediately, but can be tolerated or delayed until causes can be found to eventually eliminate the pain, rather than temporarily suppressing it through drugs.

In an article entitled "The Failure of the Modern Experiment and the Use of Psychotropic Drugs," (Lux, 1999), Kenneth Lux states:

> The toll of modern life is a result of all the features of modern life that we have described. Even in its most commonly accepted clinical form it is described as "stress," which is certainly a matter of perception and meaning first before it becomes translated and transduced into one of chemistry. Thus, any appropriate attempt to deal with stress ought to deal with the individual's perception of his or her circumstances and the values it brings to and that have helped shape those circumstances. Instead, we find the attempt to chemically alter the nervous system, as the toll of modern life continues on unabated and unchallenged, and this is described as hope?

Social views developed out of medical-model thinking have significant impact on perceived causes and treatment of ADD-behavior problems in children. Social views include different perceptions of whether psychotherapy versus drugs are the more common, appropriate, or desirable remedies.

Whether to see a psychologist or pediatrician is a choice parents make based on their preconceived views and expectations about what to do about their child's behavior, molded by current social and medical thinking. What parents are told and what they believe can effect the outcome of whether their child's ADD behavior is resolved or expected to last a lifetime. Their pediatrician and family practitioner's views are also easily molded and shaped by the news media and popular sociological thinking on the cause of human suffering. Views on how to resolve the ADD-behavior problem can be linked to philosophically historical beliefs as well as current trends in American culture. The medicalization and drugging of American children's ADD behavior is in a sense an understandable, although ineffective social cure.

6

Temperament and Resistance

Character is simply habit long continued.

—Plutarch
(circa A.D. 100)

All phenomena of existence have mind as their precursor, mind as their supreme leader, and of mind are they made.

—Joseph-Marie de Maistre
(1800)

Learning from experience, learning from people, learning from successes and failures, learning from leaders and followers: personality is formed in these reactions to stimuli in social environments.

—James MacGregor Burns
(1918)

An individual is the end product of the decisions he has made. He who fails to make decisions, for the consequences of which he is responsible, is not a person. The ego, the self, the personality—call it what you will—comes into being and grows through the process of making responsible decisions.

—Thomas Szasz
(1963)

The conflict between what one is and who one is expected to be touches all of us. And sometimes, rather than reaching for who one could be, we chose the comfort of the failed role, preferring to be the victim of circumstance, the person who didn't have a chance.

—Merle Shain
(1989)

Working psychologically with parents of ADD-behaviored children requires the ability of a clinician, and eventually the parent, to listen to all their uniqueness without needing to foreclose the assessment process with a rush toward diagnostic definitiveness or certainty. To tolerate the unpleasant thoughts and feelings in a therapeutic relationship not only promotes an improved reflectivity and non-ADD skills (behavior) on the part of parents, but serves the purpose of attaching new insight or information associated with the awareness of strong feelings or thoughts to shed new light on the causes of the child's ADD behavior. I believe what holds some therapists back from completely eliminating or resolving the ADD-behavior problem and being able to remold and reshape parents' and eventually a child's ability to be non-ADD is an inability to utilize the psychotherapeutic process to its fuller power. A parent will not be able to remold their own behavior or their child's unless there is some awareness of emotional conflicts unconscious or hidden from their awareness. Pediatrician Larry Diller (1998) states in his experience, "So often parents told me 'we tried but. . . .' I'm certain they believe they *have* tried it, yet by observing their child's unabating poor behavior I must conclude that they did not try with enough immediacy, intensity, or consistency for that child. There's a good chance that one or both parents have problems themselves with organization and following through."

I believe there is a point at which giving parents advice, setting up a behavior modification plan, or telling parents what to do otherwise, is limited. There are simply unconscious, or unknown, factors that play a part in whether parents will be able to carry out our good advice and intentions. An insight-oriented psychotherapy approach strives to develop knowledge of what else causes parents to lose motivation or stick-to-it-ness. Most people can stay on a diet for a while, but lasting dietary changes come about through understanding and changing thoughts and feelings that cause bad habits to occur.

Let me give you an example of this in a recent family situation I was working on. A mother and father complained their son was singing too much in class. He would get in trouble for humming or making various musical sounds at times when he was to be quiet. The child was described as too noisy too often, a chatterbox of sorts. The parents noticed when the child had been taking Ritalin for many years this problem seemed to be of less concern, but worsened when they stopped giving him Ritalin and began therapy. After a month or two I asked them if anybody in the family sang. Mom's immediate response was a rather quizzical, "No, none of us are going around singing all the time." To this I said, are you sure? Nobody else makes any noises? Then we began to find that the child and the rest of their family often sang in the car or at least listened to music on the radio regularly. They sang a lot while listening to the radio in the car, but they did not think this was related. His brother sang in the shower all the time. Since early childhood to get the child to go to sleep at night, his parents would have a noisy ceiling fan on and some kind of noise from either the radio or perhaps tapes with songs every night. In fact, during the day, the child had screamed so loud as an infant he developed cysts in his throat, which their doctor stated were caused by the screaming. Then we found out that the mother herself had to have music on, like the radio or TV, to get to sleep. She had to have a noisy fan on at night. The special education teacher suggested that the child sign up for chorus. Perhaps he had a certain musical temperament. They joked about his growing up to be a musician.

We talked about learning to approve and reinforce appropriate singing at certain circumstances, and how they were to punish or correct singing at inappropriate times. We talked about how they needed to pay more attention to when singing was appropriate and when singing wasn't appropriate. More specifically, we talked about when noise was appropriate or needed and when it wasn't. This seemed to be helpful and would be a reasonably good behavior modification technique. However, that suggestion and intervention, like many others, would fall short eventually without further understanding the need for singing in this child and, more importantly, the need for singing and noise in general within the family.

We found out eventually the mother needed something to soothe herself at night and at other situations during the day. In fact to this child, his singing was a way of soothing or calming himself down. There was also a need to soothe and calm his mother down. His mother had problems of insecurity, tension, and fear of being alone. She required her children to sleep with her in bed at night when the father was away on business trips. Mother and father both stated that when the father was gone frequently earlier in the child's life, the father was unable to help out with discipline and support mom emotionally and reinforce discipline.

Mother was too insecure and would not punish or reward the singing behavior and other ADD behaviors sufficiently. She referred to herself by saying, "I know I'm too much of a wimp," when it came to her son's behavior. She had to learn to become more self-confident, secure, less depressed, and stronger willed to let her son know she was in charge. A significant part of the therapy in resolving the child's ADD behavior also involved the father's increased contact with the child and a lot more at-home time. His influence in making the child "shape up" went a long way toward resolution of the child's ADD behavior. Both parents had been too lax in their discipline, not just the mother. But mother was going to be unable to carry out any of the behavioral modification plans or suggestions until she felt more self-confident. That took many, many months of therapy to focus on her own passivity in her parenting. This focus required her to become aware of painful memories and experiences in her earlier life that had blocked her awareness of the various causes of her child's singing behavior.

There is often a significant breakthrough point in psychotherapeutic work with parents, which is the juncture at which those who assume a biological or genetic deterministic notion fall short. Developing further human (parental) choice and capacity to change can uniquely occur in effective psychotherapeutic relationships in a clinician's office. It can occur at other times in life at those moments when someone is capable of experiencing a painful time in their life and eventually learn from that painful experience. Unfortunately, what I think happened psychologically in the field of ADD research and practice is an inability to go that extra distance. Those children who are unable to be psychotherapeutically changed end up being the same children whom some individuals describe as "true ADD." Remember the question is not whether a child has ADD, because all children have ADD earlier in their lives. The question is better posed as "Why is my child still ADD and how can we teach them to be non-ADD?" Because of a failure of clinicians, parents, and society to enact changes in these ADD-behaviored children, the only logical conclusion in some people's minds is that the children are simply born with a different "temperament" or "that's their personality."

The first few years of a child's life is characterized by many cognitive and behavioral changes. The cognitive process of egocentricity has been well documented in studies by Swiss developmentalist Jean Piaget. Normal child development involves a perceptual limitation to acknowledging the existence of other objects. During the first few years there is development of the external world, symbolic representations of other objects, images and thoughts of objects not immediately present. Initially there is an inability to develop differing points of view about problems, or reasons why something occurs. A lack of reflectivity exists and impulsivity predominates.

In toddlers there exists little other than what is solely in their immediate minds. An emotional self-centeredness can be depicted when a child appears distressed when asked to share and may defensively utter the word "mine!" Frequent grabbing of appealing objects from other children reveals a sense of ownership. When objects are taken there is an equally distressed reaction. Disregard for danger and pain leaves parents with the sense that toddlers have a sense of omnipotence about them.

At some point a parent and child are headed for a conflict wherein only one of them will immediately get what they want and more often than not a parent must prevail. At some point normal egocentrism and omnipotence must give way to a comfortable acceptance of rational authority and that authority is in place not to demean, but to protect and to nurture healthier and adaptive cognitive and behavioral skills.

It is a battle of wills characteristic of the terrible two's phase of development wherein much of the psychopathology of ADD/ADHD behavior develops and becomes pathological. Parent-child battles of wills are normal events at this age and inevitable as a parent intrudes upon the infant's omnipotent agenda. There is a point at which the child must give up their omnipotent illusion and overcome the inevitable separation anxiety that ensues from temporary loss of positive parental affection through discipline and the very painful realization that one doesn't always get what they want.

A child must develop a healthy respect and appreciation for a parent's authority to be eventually transferred onto other authority figures, rather than acting the way so many ADD/ADHD children do, as if what the adult has to say is relatively unimportant. Unrealized (by parent) reinforced disobedience to a parent's desires will often escalate to outright defiance, particularly if the parent is uncertain or paralyzed by guilt, or encumbered by a number of many other intrapsychic conflicts (false beliefs) and then find themselves the principal of an omnipotent tyrant.

The acceptance of a parent's rightful authority allows for improved cognitive and behavioral self-control, development of patience, containing of what seem like irresistible impulses, and a diminishing of one's egocentricity. These skills must be taught by parents who have learned how to act this way to others, and many haven't. Parents who are unable to traverse these perilous and trying times develop within themselves, if not already in existence, frustration, lack of perseverance, and lack of self-esteem.

Their own sense of parental impotence is further strengthened leading them to succumb to alternative methods of suppressing ADD/ADHD behavior in the form of a pill. By that time a parent readily seizes on the opportunity to be absolved of their parental guilt and embark upon a path of continuing to cater or succumb to a child's desires.

Parents experience considerable guilt when deciding to enter into a consulting relationship with a psychologist because their guilt often becomes resurrected. They must be held accountable for teaching their child something that they have been ill-equipped to teach previously. It is a very unsettling experience for a parent to find they have unknowingly taught ADD/ADHD behavior by failing to pass the tests of a course all parents must pass.

Parents must accept the notion that to love their child sometimes involves having to impose their will and allow the child to suffer the painful consequences of misbehavior. Some believe that if a child isn't acting naturally kind, generous, or attentive the parent isn't meeting the child's emotional needs. Then they embark upon an attempt to tailor their response to their child with the goal being alleviation of distress rather than learning. Often parents tell me they feel guilty, as if their child's protest of parental "meanness" has some basis in reality. If a child is fearful at night, lie down with them. They think that if a child is aggressive, provide them with a release. Socially unacceptable behavior cannot be met with a hint of disapproval. For other parents, imposing their disciplinary will on their child is tantamount to an act of abuse. But the pain of misbehavior must be felt by children immediately, consistently, and with effective force to motivate effective change in behavior.

A parent's own omnipotent illusion is that children should be "free" and "be allowed to be a kid." This is an egocentric disavowal of the fact that we live in a society where there are rules and norms. Rightly or wrongly none of us get our way all the time and why should a child be different? The painful consequences of distractibility, impulsivity, and hyperactivity force us to develop patience and reflectivity. ADD/ADHD is obviously a power struggle with others and a matter of ineffectively developed self-control. I find it ironic that current biopsychiatric thinking is focusing on redefining ADD/ADHD as a "primary deficit of self control" (Barkley, 1998b).

Thomas Millar's 1994 book about the "Omnipotent Child Syndrome" makes the following assertions:

> The reason there is so much violent behavior among children and youth these days is more simple than the media would have you believe. The fact is modern parents are doing a rotten job of rearing children. They have failed to lead them to normal restraint, consideration for others, and the acceptance of normal authority. Modern parents have come to believe that childhood should be constantly pleasurable, never boring or tedious. They tried hard to make it this way for their children. As a consequence the children developed neither patience nor persistence. They developed no tolerance for even minor displeasure and now when that displeasure is anger they let it all hang out with baseball bats and switchblades. By constantly catering to their desires, as the child rearing books have advised, parents have allowed children to remain so egocentric they believe that, when they close their eyes, it's night for the rest of the world. Of course they don't perceive the victim at the end of their switchblade. All they are tuned into is their own trivial frustration. By failing to discipline, parents have allowed children to retain their infantile illusions of omnipotence such that they see all authority as an unreasonable attack on their right to be wholly self-determining. When they thumb their noses at the institutions of society they truly believe they are striking a blow for freedom.

The tendency to accommodate to a child's unhealthy self-centeredness can be seen in the fervent attempt within our school system to develop individualized education plans to accommodate to a child's "special modes of learning or needs." Since when in modern psychology and education have we determined that it is the school's responsibility to spare the children the healthy pain of instruction and learning through accommodation? Self-centered children and parents are turning the modern educational system on it's head — expecting strict adherence to the Americans with Disabilities Act, charter schools, privatized education, and demands for more and more individualized services and attention. Teachers experience increasingly higher percentages of children with behavioral and learning difficulties and increasing expectations by parents and administrators to do more with less. The driving theory appears to be an increasing emphasis on parents not being held accountable to make children teachable. A child's genetic or neurobiological learning or behavioral disability justifies a parental expectation that children shouldn't be expected to sit in their seat and think. Instead we should bring them more stimulation through video screens and innovative teaching methods within an already highly and perhaps overly stimulated society.

It is not a temperamental and genetically predetermined personality trait to be inattentive, distractible, impulsive, or hyperactive, but a mode in which cognitive skill development and learning takes place in all of us. A neurologically immature or unsophisticated brain is reactive and a mature brain is reflective.

Genes are responsible for establishing the fundamental organization of the brain, but a large amount of neuronal growth that leads to establishment of connections is influenced (if not guided) by experience. One hundred thousand genes in the human genome will not determine the eventual configuration of the estimated ten trillion synaptic connections which take place during the development of cognitive skills in early childhood. Environmental experience shapes not only the content of thoughts, but also the physical structure of a child's developing brain through parental shaping/learning effects on cognitive skills of attention and reflectivity.

It's interesting to take a closer look at writings about temperament in personality research. I'm curious about some people's definition of temperament or personality. It's not unusual for ADD theorists to state temperament is something like the fussy, colicky, demanding, "virtually impossible" child to soothe or comfort in infancy. Or perhaps the "active or overactive" child from birth. Maybe temperament is the extreme of determination, intensity, sensitivity, certain types of moods, or the way a child "is." Are these "temperaments" or "personality characteristics" those psychological responses which are presumed to be genetically predetermined? Or are fussy, demanding, unhappy, overactive children responding to something in their environment or maternal responses and emotions? If someone is fussy or bouncy or overactive as an infant, do they remain that way through their life span? If someone's personality characteristic is described as shyness, does that person necessarily remain biologically constrained toward shyness their entire life as so many researchers and clinicians portray in their writings? If someone is born with a "hunter instinct" but they want to become a "gatherer", can they become at the core of their being a "gatherer"? Or is it that any of these descriptors of emotional or behavioral responses in infants are amenable to change? Can someone who has been shy as a child become non-shy? Can someone who has been fussy learn to be content? What do we make of spontaneity, creativity, playfulness, humor, easy-goingness? Are these acceptable behaviors also temperament or personality traits?

B.F. Skinner, often considered "the father" of modern behavioral psychology, in his book *Science and Human Behavior* (1953) states " . . . the doctrine of being born that way has little to do with demonstrated facts. It is usually an appeal to ignorance. 'Heredity,' as the layman uses the term, is a fictional explanation of the behavior attributed to it. . . . even when it can be shown that some aspect of behavior is due to season of birth, gross body type, or genetic constitution, the fact is of limited use. It may help us in predicting behavior, but is of little value in an experimental analysis or in practical control because such a condition cannot be manipulated after the individual has been conceived."

Psychologists tend to be labelers. We put labels on behaviors to attempt making more sense of complex, multidetermined aspects of life. Behavior is not so simple and predictable that calling behavior "temperament" is a very helpful concept when it is behavior we're trying to change. The overgeneralization often heard from parents who come to my office stating that their child has always been "a handful" or "hyperactive" since infancy often comes from hyperactive or impulsive parents. Or parents have stamped or imprinted this view of their child from early on, which became a self-fulfilling prophecy. It's no wonder that they weren't able to teach their child to be different. Parents of ADD-behaviored children who complete psychotherapy successfully become less ADD and much less of a handful themselves through the therapy change process.

So often we hear that boys are "all boy" or their excessive activity or hyperactivity is expected. Expecting it and describing it as being "all boy" most often will lead to it to continuing to occur instead of viewing it as an undesirable behavior that is present in all one- to two-year-olds and changeable.

Many parents come to my office having thought their child would just "grow out of it." This undermines the child's ability to learn to become non-ADD as parental and societal expectations have a great deal to do with shaping a child's behavior. It's not biological determinism that has caused mostly boys to become ADD-behaviored. It's likely that as families change, where mothers and fathers both work outside the home and parents are forced to share more similar psychological relationships with children, that more and more girls will become ADD-behaviored. This is something that is already being seen clinically in the last few years.

Forty years ago it was rare to see a young girl ADD-behaviored in any way, as it was almost as rare to see boys or girls ADD-behaviored. Children knew that when dad came home from work after mother repeatedly told them "Wait till you father gets home," some sort of disciplinary action would be highly likely. Teachers in my elementary school, junior high, and high school rarely had disciplinary problems in class.

I remember at my junior high school it was a big event for someone to act up. It was well known that if someone acted up, they would be marched to the P.E. coach's office where the coach's old wooden racquetball paddle with the holes in it would soon provide enough pain to the rear end to discourage any future misbehavior. There was considerably more fear of acting out than there is now. This was not an unhealthy fear of misbehaving that was simply squashing a child's innate or biologically predetermined tendency to act out, but it was the same fear that we all still possess that teaches us to make better choices in life.

Whether it be fear of something good happening or fear of something bad happening, healthy fear has its place in civilized society.

In studying parents who do not have ADD behaving children they will uniformly tell you that when they grew up, they not only had a healthy fear of their parents' authority but they also knew that punishment was reliably forthcoming. Non-ADD behaving children have developed anticipatory expectations that they are not the only one monitering their behavior.

Many times parents come to my office afraid of spanking their child because they don't want to teach their child violence. Violence and fear of discipline are two different things. Talk to most school teachers these days, and they will tell you that children seem to have little or no fear of authority or discipline. Parents are often afraid to discipline their child or impart disciplinary restrictions because their children don't "have enough time to be a kid" or have to spend all day in school or are perceived as not having enough fun in life. This is usually because both parents are already feeling like they're not having enough fun in life, having to work all day at their jobs and come home exhausted; they attempt to vicariously have more fun through their children. It's not unusual that children end up being class clowns and entertaining in school, and I see these same behaviors entertaining to parents in family therapy.

Often heard in ADD discussions on temperament is that we need to work around or adjust to a child's innate or biologically determined ways of being, i.e. change school to teach differently. This line of thinking undermines the rightful authority of schools, teachers, and ultimately parents. It gives too much power to a young child and promotes ADD behavior by excusing it. This denies the problem of a child's need to conform behavior to an adult world.

> *[There are] thousands of American children who have been affected by the rush to Ritalin. The drug's use to treat ADD has become so rampant that at the slightest sign of trouble–a child keeps running back and forth to the water fountain, has an unruly week pushing other kids on the playground, plays drums on his desk with pencils–parents are circled by the school's teachers, psychologists, and even principal, all pushing Ritalin. . .*

> *In 1990, 900,000 American kids were on Ritalin. Today an astonishing 2.5 million are – and some 80 percent of those are boys. Its use in schools has become unremarkable, nearly status quo, and therein, many caution, lies the biggest danger of all.*
>
> —Jeanie Russell, *Good Housekeeping* (1997)

After contributing to Jeanie Russell's article in the December 1997 *Good Housekeeping*, I felt a bit guilty for not also emphasizing that neither teachers nor schools are responsible for creating or solving the ADD problem. The article entitled, "The Pill That Teachers Push" could have stated more clearly that some teachers push Ritalin because their hands are tied. Yet teachers can also be very helpful by providing more emphasis on making parents more responsible and not perpetrating so much misinformation to parents. If teachers would do two things, ADD problems could be better solved: (1) Provide daily feedback to parents about an ADD-behaviored child's daily academic and behavioral performance. A very simple, quick-to-do form can be sent home by a teacher to better enable parents in therapy to get "their own progress report" and maintain more effectively what they work on in therapy. (2) Give out a more balanced and accurate representation to parents about different points of view so that what most parents get from schools is not the common medical (disease model) view of causes and treatments. Teachers tell me, "It's against school policy to make a diagnosis or recommendation." Yet they have all kinds of printed material to hand out to parents promoting medical views and treatments. I personally don't believe changing how we educate our children will solve the ADD problem until the source of the problem (parental ineffectiveness) can be eliminated.

Parents often blame the schools and teachers for not meeting the needs of their ADD-behaviored child but don't seem to realize their own responsibility to make their child "teachable." Far too often I hear parents complain about a teacher's inappropriate behavior, when it's really the parent who needs to *thank* the teacher for *any* form of discipline the teacher can provide. At times there can be too much focus on the child's needs relative to adults and society. It is not unusual for a parent to spend far more hours of their precious time negotiating with school Individualized Education Programs (IEPs), meeting with teachers, psychologically evaluating or testing their children, than they would spend in therapy fixing the problem and avoiding any "accommodations" in the long run. Society and schools can't be ruleless and bend to everybody's needs.

Temperament ceases to be a useful concept if behavior change is truly desired. To explain away a child's behavior as temperament indicates on some level acceptance of the behavior or that it's not really a problem. Often, when temperament is cited, it is a response to the parent's own conflicts pertaining to authority, both obeying (conforming) and the self-esteem necessary to impose our will upon a child. We all have to make choices about when it is our needs or someone else's that need to be met. ADD-behaving children are more self-centered than non-ADD behaving children.

A healthier view is to look at ADD behaviors as normal developmental and psychological reactions in infancy and early childhood. It is expected that a child will be interested, curious, active, moving about, and exhibiting ADD behavior because that's how they learn at that stage and become interested in the world around them. They're actively searching out, experiencing, and exploring. At that age they don't know what their limitations should be behaviorally, and it is very difficult for a child to start learning "no" and realize there are limitations in what they want to do.

The terrible two's develop because it is a time when parents have to start teaching a child to move from an ADD-behavioral response to a non-ADD behavioral response. It is not their genetically predetermined personality traits or temperament that needs to be put up with, but normal behavioral challenges to a parent to let the child know that it is no longer "king-of-the-mountain." This dethroning process is traumatic for children and parents and requires a lot of work.

The molding and shaping of non-ADD behavior occurs at this point in time. It is often helpful to point out to parents that from the time their child was two years old, there were literally thousands of moments when a parent's response determines whether that child became more ADD or less ADD. How a parent responds to a child's impulsivity, distractibility, or hyperactive behavior determines whether that child will continue to act more that way or less that way. I ask a parent to think about in any given day how many moments or "learning opportunities" or "shaping opportunities" they have to respond to a child's ADD behavior in a more effective way. Often parents find out that over the years they have engaged in behavior more likely to bring about ADD behavior than non-ADD behavior. Multiplied over many days, weeks, and years, a tremendously long-term and powerful shaping process had taken place with the parent's ADD-behaviored child that they had not even thought about in that way. Parents who are unable to effectively control their children at early ages end up having children whom society controls through special education classes, suppression and sedation of behavior through pharmaceutical methods, the court system, or the prison system.

As an undergraduate student taking psychology classes, I taught pigeons to peck green and red keys in the basement of the psychology department. That was a very useful experience in learning to shape behavior through punishments and rewards. A pigeon could be taught to act quite attentively to a green colored light if it knew it would get food for pecking that light in a variety of different behavioral patterns. The principle of reinforcing successive behavioral approximations toward the desired goal has often been a useful technique in teaching parents how to respond to a child's ADD behavior more quickly, more effectively, and repeatedly, until it becomes something the child can do on his or her own.

Shaping pigeons to peck keys is similar to shaping children to act non-ADD. That shaping process is very similar to what parents do with toddlers when they say "do this" or "don't do that." How consistently, reliably, and effectively parents do this is crucial in shaping children's behavior. Parents have numerous shaping (learning) opportunities or moments every day, every week, eighteen years of a child's life. *How* a child's behavior is shaped determines a child's habitual (temperament or personality) way of thinking, feeling, and acting. Parents shape a child's behavior one way or another, either actively, or passively by doing "nothing."

Parents often tell me that they've "used" all the techniques, punishments, rewards, charts, and behavior modification methods. In all cases, any of the usual methods would work if the parents were to use them effectively, consistently, and appropriately. I often hear parents say their child will not sit in time out. It's not that the child will just not sit in time out, but that the child won't do a lot of things because the child has very little respect or fear of the parent, and the parent has very little control over the child. Children don't pay attention to adults and respond appropriately unless we give them good reason to do so. And it's not always the threat of punishment. Children can also learn that good things happen when they pay attention, listen, and concentrate.

Parents often state, "If ADD isn't genetic, why are all my children different when I've raised them the same way?" We don't raise them the same way. There are many psychological and social influences that impinge upon children and families to shape a child's characteristic ways of behaving.

Even before a child is born, parents have different hopes, dreams, attitudes, and expectations of their child that play themselves out in how they relate to their newborn child. "Boys will be boys" or "Boys are more active" or "He's been that way since he was born." There are many differences from the time one child is born to the next. Parents have different jobs, live in different places, interact with different people, have another child or two in the family to contend with, have different lifestyles, and some have different spouses. Parents change too. I'm a psychologically different person than I was five, ten, even twenty years ago. I'm a smarter parent now, after having five children. I learned as I went along as a parent. We tend to forget about the myriad changes that take place every day in our lives. We don't even love our children equally. Parents will admit they have different feelings about each one of their children.

Parents often state, "Why should I talk about the past? It's over and done with!" Actually not. While we can't change the past, we can study and learn from it. Otherwise, why not throw out all the history books? Memories, feelings, understandings, perceptions, and attitudes are still very much in the present, and often those are what still bother us. We are troubled by things unresolved in our minds that we tend to push away, avoid, ignore, or medicate. But not learning or coming to terms with these things makes it very difficult to raise children in a less conflict-laden relationship or environment. To specifically study our learning histories with our parents, those who were our teachers, is an opportunity to reevaluate where we get stuck in trying to parent our children.

At first glance many parents don't appear "ADD" themselves. They present themselves as worried or concerned about their children and may state, "I never acted this way" or "I've never taught them to be that way" or "I have rules and values I've taught my child." Maybe not consciously, but misbehavior has often been taught unknowingly or unconsciously not necessarily through modeling, but by allowing ADD behavior to remain suppressed. A parent's rebelliousness, defiance, abdication of responsibility, laziness, forgetfulness, or inability to sit still, and lack of patience exists, but usually not the way they think about it. I often find a tremendous amount of *unconscious* acceptance of a child's ADD behavior, and on a day-to-day basis the ADD behavior isn't as troubling to them as what is expressed during the interview with me, because that's the time they're supposed to come and tell you all that's wrong. Often they'll develop insight on a solution but "forget" to carry it out during the week between appointments. Often, not until later in the therapy can a parent's "collusion" with their child's ADD behavior become apparent. Not until they trust telling you more about what they really do will faults be more willingly admitted. Parents may not at first glance view their own symptoms as similar to their child's, but the underlying problems are the same: lack of attentiveness to the solution or appropriate behavior in carrying it out. The absence of evidence is not evidence of absence.

There is no doubt in my mind that a child's temperament or personality style is something that is developed in life, and always susceptible to change and transformation with concerted effort on a parent's part. It's interesting that when I ask parents how to explain other aspects of their child's behaviors that don't seem to be the immediate focus of clinical attention, they describe the same kinds of shaping principles or behavior management responses to develop those same behaviors. They don't realize they have been doing it, or they have not chosen to pay attention to the ADD behaviors as being just as important. It is a parent's job to teach non-ADD behavior in infants and toddlers.

The most ADD-behaviored and hyperactive children I see in my office routinely come from families marked with disorganization, chaos, and inconsistencies. They are children who are either left to fend for themselves, or parental response to certain behaviors is fraught with excessive emotionality, and there is very little emotional distance in the parent at the time. It's as if the parent is unable to separate themselves from the child. There is no realization that there is a conceptually simple but difficult-to-bring-about teaching or developmental task to accomplish with their child. Instead, the child had been viewed psychologically as a sort of computer program that was to unfold all on its own after simply pushing the "birth" button.

The types of resistance to therapeutic work with parents are many and varied. Professionals who promote a disease model might think the children discussed in this book as not "true ADD," referring to certain children diagnosed with ADD that have "true biochemical or genetic causes." To this false belief, I would state that I would like to know what is a definition of "true ADD" and its behavioral manifestations?

I purposely chose to present some of the children in my book knowing that many practitioners would probably diagnose or view these children as "truer ADD" children than any others, based on the severity and nature of symptoms or problems expressed. Bobby would be arguably one of the worst ADD-behaving kids a practitioner might encounter. I knew that therapy would take some time due to the types of problems in his family. I've challenged skeptics to provide me with the "worst case" of ADD in a child they'd ever encountered, one whom they believe has a biochemical or genetic abnormality or ADD temperament, and put my therapeutic skills to the test. In Bobby's case the referring pediatrician had that in mind. He now sends me many children. Quite surprising to most parents is an additional guarantee I often give them. I will tell a skeptical parent that they're welcome to obtain a legal contract from their lawyer that I will sign, guaranteeing their child will be cured of ADD. We mutually define "cure," and parent or parents must agree to do their part. One is that they have to show up for all therapy sessions, absent any legitimate reason for missing a session. A parent has to be willing to be as honest as can be, allow their personal lives to be completely scrutinized, say everything that comes to their mind, and free associate. Lastly, they have to be willing to consider that their child's ADD can be cured and that parental responsibility for change is of absolute importance.

What typically happens, guarantee or not, is that some parents and their children choose not to come back to see me after the first session. I have noticed that a poor follow-up rate seems to hold true with most any kind of therapeutic practice, my own or someone else's. The follow-through rate with therapy for any kind of problem is unfortunately relatively poor. Poor follow-up also seems to happen in following a physician's advice to take prescription medications, stay with one's exercise program or diet, strictly adhere to traffic laws, show up at polls to vote, floss one's teeth upon the dentist's recommendation, and many other aspects of human behavior. It is not always the practitioner's treatment that is faulty as much as a parent or patient's conscious and sometimes unconscious choice, free will, or lack of control over their life that may sabotage successful treatment.

Those who philosophically believe that we are victims of biochemical disturbances, genetic abnormalities, or any other forces external to a human being's conscious mind may have a difficult time accepting therapy. I question the skeptics' view of ADD being incurable and ask them to examine their own parent-child relationships with their children or their own parents. At what point do we draw a line in the sand to determine what we're responsible for in our child's psychological development, our relationship with our own parents, and people in general?

Closer scrutiny of someone's beliefs about what causes children to do what they do will often end up with a parent struggling with how much they potentially have control over their child's behavior versus other forces. Individual and societal abdication of responsibility for human behavior is of central interest and a topic worthy of discussion when solving ADD behavior problems.

7
Parenting Works

Love your children, care about them, respect them, do as much as possible to have them grow and develop, teach them social skills, and teach them how to identify and express their feelings and to become uniquely human; but at the same time, care about them enough and love them enough to give them guidance, structure, limits, and control as they need it.

—Michael R. Valentine, educator
How To Deal With Difficult Discipline Problems (1988)

Parents are blamed, but not trained. Millions of new mothers and fathers take on a job each year that ranks among the most difficult anyone can have, taking an infant, a little person who is almost totally helpless, assuming full responsibility for his physical and psychological health and raising him so he will become a productive, cooperative, and contributing citizen. What more difficult and demanding job is there? Yet, how many parents are trained for it?

—Thomas Gordon
P.E.T.: Parent Effectiveness Training (1997)

Good families—even great families—are off track 90 percent of the time! The key is that they have a sense of destination. They know what the "track" looks like. And they keep coming back to it time and time again.

—Stephen R. Covey
The 7 Habits of Highly Effective Families (1997)

> *What distinguishes effective from ineffective caregiving? Scientists have identified two fundamental aspects of caregiving that are particularly important for children's adjustment. The first concerns how much warmth, nurturance, and acceptance (versus hostility and rejection) caregivers convey to children. The second concerns how much control, structure, and involvement (versus permissiveness and detachment) caregivers display toward children.*
>
> —National Advisory Mental Health Council (1995)

It is important for parents to realize they can cure their child's ADD problem. Just because they don't see a solution after all they've tried, it doesn't mean a solution doesn't exist. The psychotherapy process is a health-oriented positive search for information that is not just out of a parent's awareness, but initially the therapist also. The therapist knows how to find the missing pieces of a puzzle, but doesn't know what the pieces will all look like until the therapy process unfolds.

We are looking to discover the cures and not the disease. We are not giving up and assuming the cure is out of our hands. Therapy, difficult as it is, becomes a very positive growing experience for parents. There is too much pessimistic and fatalistic thinking in American psychology and psychiatry, which has done nothing helpful to solve the ADD problem by being fixated on "diseases," "sicknesses," "temperaments," or "drugs." These concepts lead us away from what seems to be common sense.

It is common to identify anything but parents as causes of ADD behavior these days. One popular book recently stated parents have virtually no significant effect on the psychological growth and development of children. The author states "Do parents have any important long-term effects on the development of their child's personality? No." (Harris 1998)

The mental health profession has been criticized recently by past American Psychological Association (APA) president Martin Seligman as being too negativistic. A recent edition of the *American Psychologist* was a special issue on "Happiness, Experience, and Optimal Human Functioning." Seligman (2000) points out:

> A science of positive subjective experience, positive individual traits, and positive institutions promises to improve quality of life and prevent the pathologies that arise when life is barren and meaningless. The exclusive focus on pathology that has dominated so much of our discipline results in a model of the human being lacking the positive features that make life worth living. Hope, wisdom, creativity, future-mindedness, courage, spirituality, responsibility, and perseverance are ignored or explained as transformations of more authentic negative (chemical) impulses. The fifteen articles in this millennial issue of the *American Psychologist* discuss such issues as what enables happiness, the effects of autonomy and self-regulation, how optimism and hope affect health, what constitutes wisdom, and how talent and creativity come to fruition. The authors outline a framework for a science of positive psychology, point to gaps in our knowledge, and predict that the next century will see a science and [a] profession that will come to understand and build the factors that allow individuals, communities, and societies to flourish.

Dr. Seligman has pointed out before that therapy works. Parents might not get that impression from today's media and their consulting doctors or teachers. In his article (Seligman 2000) he goes on to state: "Practitioners went about treating the mental illnesses of patients within a disease framework by repairing damage: damaged habits, damaged drives, damaged childhoods, and damaged brains."

Practioners sometimes focus on damages and not the repair work. There is an emphasis on what is lacking, not what needs to be develped or created.

Research in child development has shown over and over the importance of parents and early childhood influences. Sometimes we take this for granted. Parents need to be supported and nurtured to realize they are more powerful and capable than they thought. That it's okay to sit down and take the time to evaluate all their inadequacies. They're only human. To enable them, empower them once a week to learn to act differently with their children in therapy is a powerful motivator. Especially when they learn that to change themselves is the greatest gift they could ever give to their children. You've seen other parents act too lenient, too harsh, too passive, too active, inconsistent, too controlling, too smothering, too giving, etc., etc. You've thought in your mind what you would do differently and what that other parent should do differently. The behavioral solution is most often obvious. Do you ever notice how you can see more clearly the deficits in other parents, but why you are so fuzzy about your own children? Therapy defogs our eye glasses.

A better approach to solving the ADD problem is to consider that ADD behavior is learned or developed within the parent-child relationship. This line of reasoning considers that the way a parent and child relate could have something to do with causing the child's behavior. Many research studies show that inattentiveness, hyperactivity, and impulsivity can be behaviorally changed into attentiveness, reflectivity, and calmness. Many experienced mental health practitioners who have worked with children and families on the ADD problem know that psychological methods can solve ADD problems. There are many medical practitioners who recommend psychological methods of changing ADD behavior, and often Ritalin is not considered to be the primary treatment modality but is prescribed in conjunction with outpatient psychological treatment focused on behavior change. Many pediatricians will prescribe Ritalin or other drugs contingent on a parent seeking counseling or psychotherapy. Good books on effective parenting have been available for a long time. Some that can be very helpful to parents include a recent book entitled *Ritalin Is Not the Answer* by David Stein (1999). This book provides many practical suggestions for teachers and parents to follow and is easy and enjoyable to read. Books by John Rosemond (1993) about affirmative parenting give a lot of helpful information to parents. A series of videotapes by Michael Valentine (1988) also provides hands-on techniques for parents.

Many parents are given the impression that the entire field of psychology has reached the consensus that ADD behavior problems are medically caused and treated. In reality, there are many books and articles written by various authors representing viewpoints and practices consistent with those in this book. In a recent article Rea Reason (1999) described a report from the British Psychological Society addressing current controversies about

ADD. In the review of research entitled "ADHD: A Psychological Response to an Evolving Concept," she determined the following:

> The nature of the research has required controlled experimental conditions rather than the natural settings of home or classroom. Generalizability and validity can therefore be questioned. There is a need for corroborative studies involving parents, teachers, and the children themselves, to demonstrate that the hypothesized mechanisms provide plausible and valid explanations in the real world. The great majority of children considered to have ADHD do not have a history of neurobiological damage and are found to have no neurological signs on examination.
>
> Children's happiness and success depend on their constructive response to the expectations of family, friends, and school. Difficulties in meeting these kinds of demands inevitably have a range of social, educational, and psychological consequences for the child. These will almost certainly be compounded by personal unhappiness.
>
> Although most children meet the demands (with varying degrees of effort) a minority do not. Their problems may be rooted in many factors, including developmental delay, a lack of compliance in relation to authority, poor peer relationships, or emotional difficulties associated with family circumstances.

A series of articles on "Biased Maternal Reporting of Child Psychopathology" appeared in the October 1998 issue of the Journal of the American Academy of Child and Adolescent Psychiatry. Pediatrician Joseph Jacobs (1998) stated,

> In the literature on attention deficit hyperactivity disorder (ADHD) rarely does one find assessments of fathers. While it has become 'fashionable' to write of the need to deal with the

> behavioral components and the family, it is virtually assumed that symptoms result from ADD and not from the family. Hence, it is the child who is 'labeled and treated.' There is very little attempt in psychiatric history taking to explore the psychosocial history of the parents and grandparents. What is the effect on a child if a parent has chronic headaches? Where does one read of the family background of the parents? Did the latter belong to a close family? Was growing up a good experience? To whom did they talk - their mother, their father, or neither? What form of discipline was used in their families of origin? Was it the use of a belt, being spanked, being shouted at or put down? Did their family of origin have one or more alcoholic beverages? Does the child behave differently with mother or father?

In my reading of the total number of articles published in professional journals these questions are investigated or considered in about 5% of them. One has to wonder if the search for biological causes is a sign of the times to accommodate to a lack of time and patience, the best way to justify one's professional existence, or perhaps the best funded line of research?

A recent critical appraisal of published systematic reviews and meta-analysis on ADD/ADHD (Jadad et al. 1999) points out considerable flaws in the research on assessment and course of treatment. They state, "None of the reviews appear to capture information on family characteristics, family structure, socioeconomic status, maternal education, paternal education, family functioning, or parental depression. There was no mention of family related outcomes (for example, parental skills, parental confidence, parental adjustment, family functioning) in any of the reviews.

Coming to a mental health practitioner can often be viewed as something of a psychoanalysis wherein people go in and lay on the analyst's couch and free associate. Psychoanalysis has for many years stood in a precarious position related to neurobiology. From the beginning of the work of Sigmund Freud, who initially ceded primacy to organic (medical) factors and later defined the scope of psychoanalysis as covering all which could not be explained biologically, there has been a continual increase in looking at both biological and nonbiological causes of psychological problems in life. Morrell (1998) points out there has been increased knowledge in neurochemistry and brain anatomy, with improved techniques for study, and a growing acceptance of a perspective which maintains that all "mental disorders" can be understood neurobiologically and that the treatment of these disorders stems primarily from a psychopharmacological or medication perspective. From this standpoint, talk therapy is seen primarily as a supplement to medical treatment. Talk therapy is then seen as serving the function of helping people accept the fact of their having a brain disease or disorder, and they need to be helped to adapt to this objective reality in their life. At best from this perspective, therapy is seen as helping people undo or change behavioral patterns developed in trying to cope with their "illness" or "disease" prior to the advent of future, more appropriate medical (drug) treatments. From this medical view, therapy is viewed as inherently cognitive and behavioral in nature, and psychoanalytically-oriented approaches looking more at emotional processes and their associations are irrelevant at best as well as potentially antitherapeutic in the sense that this process might lead a doctor or patient away from "real treatment." Therapy is seen by many people as simply a way to help a child cope, the parents cope with the child, or build "self-esteem." Even using medical terms like "disease," "disorder," or "cure" implies ADD is a medical problem.

One must be willing to consider there is a fundamental difference in belief among people about why we act the way we do. Is it something genetically or neurochemically induced or is our behavior something that is learned and developed based on the way we relate to other people or other people relate to us? Many people believe that children have to be *taught* to pay attention, to listen, and to act calmly. A problem in proposing that ADD is a learned behavior is that parents are referred to a psychologist and psychological methods are recommended. Sometimes ADD can become a tolerable "reason" for parents to obtain help, as if there has to be a socially agreed-upon "diagnosis" or problem for someone to seek help outside the family. Most mental health practitioners know that the most frequent parent referral question is, "Does my child have ADD?" rather than the more useful question, "Can you help us find out why our child isn't paying attention in school and show us how to help our child do so?" Parents often become angry, confused, or defensive about the notion that they have somehow caused the ADD behavior problem in their child. Sometimes people even go so far as to say that mental health practitioners just want to "blame the parents" for everything.

The controversy about ADD is caused by differing beliefs about how we become who we are. Some might consider it a "fact of life" that as parents, we have the responsibility to teach our children "good or appropriate behavior" and sometimes unknowingly we teach our children "bad or inappropriate behavior." Most parents would also agree that we as parents try to love our children as best we can, but that none of us as parents is so perfect or psychologically well-adjusted or skilled as to be able to go through life producing perfectly well-behaved children. Nevertheless, we can try to do better and continue to improve our parental relationship with our children. I think most parents would agree that when we have noticed problems in our own life, or problems with our children in particular, the cause of the problems has often gone unnoticed or remained unknown to us until it's been pointed out. It is as if we have blinders on about some aspects of our behavior with our children.

These blind spots very often get pointed out in families where there has been a divorce, and the new stepparent points out to the biological or custodial parent that there is something amiss with the child's behavior. In non-divorced families parents are most often confronted with someone from their child's school recommending an evaluation for ADD.

It is important for parents to realize that it is not "all their fault" that their child may act ADD, but it is their responsibility to do something about it. There have been very significant changes historically in families. We now have predominantly two-parent wage earners. Expected roles of mothers and fathers toward their children are changing. Fathers are now expected to play a somewhat different role in relationship to their children, because now most mothers are wage earners outside the home. The divorce rate now exceeds 50 percent. More sophisticated technology for communication tends to emphasize quickness. Often parents complain they just do not have enough time to do everything that needs to be done. Society demands quicker and more immediate solutions to problems. These changes in families have caused attention to be placed on working and "doing," rather than on listening and spending time together. It is very difficult for people to consciously schedule time to sit and talk to each other; and further, not just to talk but to listen deeply and search for causes of problems even though the causes are not readily apparent. Nowadays we pick something up at a fast food restaurant while we're whisking our children to baseball or soccer practice or someplace else, after mom and dad have been working eight hour days and have just enough time to pick up the kids and get them to bed in the evening. More and more we are a hyperactive culture. Everything is faster: mail, airplanes, food service, telephones, computers, cars, athletes, our doctor office visits, even the ability to wage and win wars. We have put a price on quickness. Time is of the essence in more ways than one. Attention, reflectivity, and calmness are those behavioral aspects we seek in our children whom we diagnose as ADD, yet we are unconsciously or unknowingly producing the opposite in our children because we are really acting ADD ourselves.

When someone is willing to sit down in a psychologist's office for an hour a week and contemplate or discuss deeply why their child is acting a certain way, wonderful changes can happen. One can then pay attention to those factors that seem to be related to a child paying attention versus not paying attention. Inconsistencies in parents and how they relate to the child, significant differences in discipline, even significant values about how a child is supposed to act come forth and can be discussed as causing a child to act ADD. When parents do this, there is always obvious evidence that a child's ADD behavioral changes are under psychological or environmental (parental) control.

Effective psychological work on ADD problems in children involves working with families and parents to teach or allow parents to discover on their own appropriate discipline, consistency, and behavior change techniques. It often involves taking a look at psychological problems within the parents or maybe even their marriage. Many parents have learned that when they sit down long enough to talk to each other about how to raise their children, behavior change can occur. Those parents who sit down and try to change the child's behavior to make them less ADD sometimes do not know how to do that, or maybe it's one of those blind spots getting in the way. Parents can wisely accept the concept that just because they don't see the answers doesn't mean the answers do not exist. It's like psychological detective work to eventually solve the mystery of why a child really acts ADD. Parents have been pleased to know that the cause of their child's ADD behavior is a result of simply not realizing something or paying attention to certain aspects of their parental relationship with their child. Different ways of responding to a child can be discovered, and the ADD behavior problem goes away.

It is interesting to study the reasons why many people still search for a biochemical or genetic cause of ADD. One reason is that as small children, we are very often trained that when something hurts or bothers us, we look to the medical or physiological cause and cure. Sitting down and talking about changing our children's behavior takes a lot of time and sometimes costs a lot of money. Prescription pills are relatively cheaper, quick, immediately effective, and don't require all the hours and hours of parental change and revelation of our previously unknown and feared flaws to someone else. It's very scary for a person to admit that maybe they do not have complete control over their own behavior and that there could be something unknown or unconscious in them that is causing problems in their child. People generally do not take kindly to someone suggesting that maybe they are doing something wrong. It can be a very bitter pill to swallow, but sometimes the search for truth hurts.

My wife volunteered to teach art education at Vacation Bible School last summer. One morning she noticed a small child looking as if she didn't feel very well. The child came up to her and said she had a stomach ache and felt bad. My wife's initial reaction was to perhaps call the child's mother to have the child picked up and taken home, have the child see a nurse, or perhaps even go see the doctor for a medical evaluation for some sort of medication, or perhaps bed rest. Then she reminded herself that many physical problems are actually psychologically based and perhaps something else was bothering this little girl. She asked the little girl if there was something bothering her, and the girl shook her head and said, "No, my tummy hurts." My wife asked her again if there was something bothering her, worrying her, or maybe she was upset about something. The girl still shook her head and said, "No, my tummy hurts." My wife decided to ask the little girl if she would like to join her and help her clean up markers and crayons. The little girl seemed interested. Then suddenly a few minutes later the little girl came over to my wife, climbed in her lap, and started to cry. She sobbed about her worry whether her mother would come back and how she was an only child. Essentially she missed her mother. My wife and the little girl continued to talk. Then the little girl's face brightened up and she appeared happy and her stomach ache went away. For the rest of the afternoon she was stomach pain free.

With my own children my wife and I try to apply the very same things I tell parents in my office. Whenever we're with our children we have to study and observe whether we're behaving or responding to our children in a manner likely to produce ADD behavior or non-ADD behavior. When our children are too active, they have to slow down. When interrupting my wife or me, they're told to wait. When too loud, they're told to quiet down. Any other ADD behavior is met with an immediate response to produce a healthier, more acceptable non-ADD behavior. When told to do something, they're expected to do it each and every time, immediately and correctly without complaint. If spoken to, they're expected to look at us, listen, and respond appropriately. At the same time, throughout the day, they are appreciated, loved, listened to, respected, rewarded, and anything else that produces non-ADD behavior on their part. This needs to occur until the child develops their own ability to respond similarly to others the same way, on their own and automatically. Our children are expected to develop the same habits, values, morals, and ways of behaving as we do. Excuses are not tolerated. Sincere apologies are accepted, but corrective behavior still has to occur.

We are in charge of our children, not the other way around. Our family is not a democracy when our children are one, two, or three years of age. When they have learned to be non-ADD, their desires and needs are given more weight. Only then are their options, freedom, choices, and preferences given more consideration. These types of dynamics do not occur with enough frequency or consistency in ADD-behaviored children and their families.

We are far from being perfect parents, but we must demand of ourselves as parents to take responsibility for how our children behave, more than anybody or anything else in life. Of my five children, the oldest is more ADD-behaved than my youngest, only because of what my wife and I have learned over the years. How my children behave has nothing to do with their inborn "temperament" or "personality," but it has everything to do with my wife's and mine. When my children exhibit ADD behavior, I try to be the first one to not only blame myself, but to hold myself responsible for finding a solution and teaching my children to do the same. When parents of an ADD-behaving child start telling me all of the other reasons for their child's behavior, I listen but try to make sure one way or another that the parent accepts ultimate responsibility.

8
My Personal Experience

I have been a clinical child psychologist for eighteen years. I've read numerous journal articles, books, and other written commentaries on attention deficit disorder. I have read about the causes, treatments, and effects of this problem. I have worked clinically with children in inpatient and outpatient settings. I have been an expert witness in legal proceedings where one parent disagrees with the other about medicating their child or whether the most helpful treatment is being administered. I have published a series of research studies in peer-reviewed journals on the assessment of ADD beginning with my doctoral dissertation on the subject to now (Carter, Zelko, Oas, and Waltonen 1990; Fantino, Case, and Oas 1981; Oas 1983; 1984a, 1984b, 1985a, 1985b, 1985c). I conduct ongoing literature searches on ADD. I receive referrals from schools, parents, the Social Security Administration, Office of Vocational Rehabilitation, various types of physicians, and other sources concerning a particular child's ADD. In all, I have evaluated thousands of children who over the years are considered to have ADD. I also have five children of my own.

I have successfully treated all children whose parent(s) were willing to engage in weekly family psychotherapy, parent counseling, or individual therapy for one of the parents to the point when the child was no longer ADD. "Cure" is defined, and applies to the children studied in this book, as children who at the end of treatment (1) received A's and B's in regular or mainstream classes, (2) no longer received notes from the school about misbehavior, (3) no longer take Ritalin or any psychotropic medication, (4) were moved out of special education and no longer considered "learning" or "behavior disabled," (5) were rated by teachers, parents, their doctor, and anyone else as non-ADD, (6) would be described as "normal" by most anyone's definition, (7) no longer exhibited any of their presenting problems of ADD or other problems of concern that existed at the start of their parents' therapy, and (8) after years of follow-up with parents none of these criteria changed, i.e. the child remained non-ADD. Of parents who seek only "partial" cures, a child will improve to varying degrees limited only by parental desire to terminate treatment at some point. Some parents choose to leave therapy grateful that their ADD-behaviored child improved, wanting to finish the work on their own.

I have focused the majority of my work on parents of the ADD-behaviored child rather than working individually with the ADD-behaviored child. Often parents find this to be unusual or troubling because they have expectations that I'm going to do something with or to their child that they have been unable to do or want to do themselves. It's not unusual that after an initial evaluation and contact with a child that I rarely see the child again. Many parents for various reasons choose not to come back. Psychotherapy is a very difficult choice for a parent to make. While this seems different from the way many mental health practitioners approach the ADD problem, and quite different from many parents' expectations, it makes a lot of sense when one understands that parents are responsible for changing themselves and their child.

I have sometimes seen parents with the child in therapy because they have a need to bring the child. This has allowed us at times to witness problems and work more specifically in a behavioral approach to improve our understanding of the problem and/or suggest different parental responses. This typically is done in families where initially the parents have more trouble with talking or free associating (saying whatever comes to their mind), or the parents can't accept at that point that they are completely responsible for their children. They may feel they have a mistaken idea that if the child is not present, their child is being ignored or neglected. Even with those families where the child actually comes to therapy, most of the time it's not unusual for the parents to continue to do the talking and free associating during the session. Often the child does not come back in with the parent or parents. Often the psychopathology of the parents needs more focused attention, and sometimes there are issues discussed that don't necessarily need to be brought up in the presence of the child. Particularly when a "free associative process" is being utilized to a more full extent, a lot of sensitive information comes out. A parent's relationship with the child is different from that of the spouse with whom free associative material is more appropriately discussed.

I have been in full-time independent clinical practice and have seen a wide range of children over the years. For a few years I had the unique opportunity of evaluating more than five hundred ADD children in and around a very large military hospital, receiving referrals from pediatricians, family practitioners, and other individuals. I psychologically tested and evaluated hundreds of children referred with the instruction "Rule out ADD." A lot of interesting patterns were apparent on psychological tests administered, quite supportive of my conclusions of the ADD problem. Many parents have seen me not knowing what my "orientation" was. I've worked with so called "motivated" or "psychologically-minded parents" and "nonmotivated" or "nonpsychologically-minded parents." I have a lot of objective and subjective data related to the ADD problem with many children.

My experiences have led me to some important conclusions about the nature of the ADD problem. The majority of publicized opinion, particularly in the mental health field, is that ADD is some kind of brain dysfunction, chemical imbalance, or genetic abnormality in etiology. Some say ADD has both a medical or neurological cause and a psychosocial cause. The predominant treatment approach has been either prescription medications like Ritalin, Adderall, Concerta, Wellbutrin, Cylert, or Dexedrine, or even anti-convulsants like Depakote or Tegretol. Newer drugs continue to come out. Many people combine drugs with some kind of psychological intervention or therapy. I have found that thinking of the ADD problem as caused by something medical or neurological, and treated primarily or exclusively with drugs, has rarely if ever been helpful in bringing about the healthier solutions that most parents truly want when they come to see me.

There is no clinical proof or evidence that ADD has anything to do with a child's brain from a nonpsychological perspective. Most research studies have not evaluated children in real life or private practitioner's office settings rather than clinic, agency, or research settings. Empirical or scientific research also has the problem of accounting for individual differences among children and their families.

Parents are often surprised to find their child can be accurately diagnosed ADD in about thirty seconds just by explaining what the "official" diagnostic criteria are. A lot of money and resources go into the mistaken notion that ADD requires a comprehensive diagnostic effort beyond a careful history-taking interview. There is a disagreement about causes, and one's beliefs about causes dictates what one does in their assessment. For example, it is often heard that there is "true ADD" versus ADD caused by other things. Those who believe in a "true ADD" think it's a medical or neurological problem. A lot of effort is spent trying to evaluate the problem through psychological tests, parent and teacher reports, behavior rating scales, and medical and physical history taking as if it's important to decide what "true ADD" is as opposed to ADD caused by nonmedical factors.

What is underemphasized and quite unsupported is the parents' ability to learn how to teach their child how to pay attention, concentrate, and act non-ADD. Any time a parent is willing to consistently and reliably come in and talk about their parental relationship with a child and focus specifically on issues of discipline, consistency, stability, predictability, calmness, and responsibility, ADD behaviors eventually cease to exist in their entirety as a clinical problem.

Most parents who have two-year-old children know from experience that their child is ADD and needs to be taught to listen, pay attention, act calmly, and think about the consequences of their actions. Most parents intuitively know that prescription of medications isn't the most helpful approach for their child but they feel desperate. Most parents know that more effective parenting is the key to a child's ADD behavior problem, but it's difficult to acknowledge this and do something about it. Human beings tend to be lazy, not do everything they know they should, and have difficulty starting things and following through. It's especially difficult to assume personal responsibility for bad things that happen to us in life.

Think about the ways in which the overweight problem in America is addressed. There is a lot of money spent on research looking for the obesity gene, looking at hormonal factors, heredity factors, stomach stapling, fad diets, and most every imaginable method of achieving weight loss other than simply eating less, eating healthier foods, and exercising more. I often give parents the analogy that coming to psychotherapy is like signing up for gym class for a weight problem. Changes are possible, and if they show up and attempt to go through the exercises once a week, they're probably going to lose weight. In a way, therapy is similar. I often function as someone's psychological cheerleader as we go through mental aerobics. Much of the effort working with ADD parents and children is to develop and reinforce the notion in a parent's mind that we are psychologically much more capable of changing than we give ourselves credit for. A lot of work is involved in building parents' self-confidence and capability to tackle the normal developmental tasks of teaching children, who are all by nature ADD, to become socially non-ADD beings.

It is reasonable to assume that all human behavior has a neurobiological correlate. From one perspective, all behavior is based upon the functioning of neural cells and neurotransmitters conveying messages between themselves. Therefore, ADD and other human behavior, as well as emotions like anger or happiness, awareness of pain, choice of whom to root for in the Super Bowl, have neural correlates. This does not mean that genes cause all these things. Without brain cells or neurotransmission, people cannot think or feel at all. To that degree, causes of ADD based on a medical or genetic level of analysis is a separate issue from parental or environmental causes. Psychopharmacologists will tell you that at the level of cellular changes in the brain, environmental effects can alter genetic material in cells. Genetic and environmental influences go both ways in a circular fashion, not in a linear fashion.

In David Stein's 1999 book entitled *Ritalin Is Not the Answer: A Drug-Free, Practical Program for Children Diagnosed With ADD or ADHD,* he reviews the literature on ADD and concludes: "I believe that all bodily or brain changes that have ever been measured in ADD or ADHD children are the result of their environment and therefore are disorders and not diseases. Disorders can be treated behaviorally, without the need for medication."

Some day the field of neurology could become so sophisticated that it might discover that every thought or emotion, healthy or unhealthy, has a corresponding biochemical change in the body. Even more interesting are many studies in medicine and psychology that provide some evidence that thoughts and feeling can effect changes in the physical or neurological functioning of the human body. In other words, how we think and how we feel can do just the opposite, change how our physical body functions. Common examples of this would be chronic headaches or stomach problems that are considered to be "stress-related." We know meditation changes the body physically, and we know that we can also become physiologically aroused because of thought.

I've found some information about ADD to be particularly threatening to mental health practitioners, especially those who make a lot of money through prescribing medications or do extensive testing and don't know how to do effective parent therapy or family therapy. One's professional reputation and beliefs about the nature of being human is called into question. I've found when trying to engage in discussions with other mental health professionals about the ADD issue, they cite "research evidence" for their biological or medical views, but they're very inexperienced or intolerant of actually looking at specific studies and discussing the strengths and limitations. I find parents to be much more willing to listen to different sides of the story and more eager to get information from both perspectives. When parents tell me about the research evidence for ADD being a medical problem, I might ask them to bring me the actual study—especially those studies behind the fancy colored pictures of an "ADD child's brain" that have never been replicated or validated.

Unfortunately there's a relative lack of research looking into parental and family therapy cures and causes for ADD. Mental health practitioners, private psychotherapists in particular, many of whom are successful in solving ADD behavior problems in children, tend to not publish their work. Practitioners have relatively less incentive to take the time to publish their work to provide better education about how to solve the ADD problem. This lack of clinical data has been one of my motivations to publish this book. The increasing misinformation presented to me in my office every day by parents troubles me. I have chosen to provide information that seems to be considerably lacking in the professional literature. In this book there are several case studies and samples of successful ADD treatment with parents who have solved the ADD behavior problem. I have presented a variety of ADD case scenarios, with children ranging from very severely hyperactive, impulsive, and inattentive, to relatively mild and intermittent problems of ADD which were relatively more easily and quickly resolved. Even children with an obvious neurological problem such as mental retardation, or children who have been diagnosed autistic should not be considered untreatable. All children can be taught to be non-ADD.

ADD is a diagnosis that can cover a wide variety of children's daily behavioral activities. It can be expressed as aggressiveness and defiance, or be diagnosed in children who can sit still and are not hyperactive, or in children who are constantly in motion and cannot sit still. The defining characteristics of the diagnosis are very broad. Many children come to my office, labeled as exhibiting ADD behaviors, only to act very non-ADD in my office or in the presence of a particular parent. I point out to parents that their ADD child certainly has the capacity to be non-ADD when engaged in Nintendo or Sega games. More recently with the Pokemon fad, parents are often surprised when I point out that their child can learn all the one hundred plus Pokemon characters' qualities and strengths. An ADD child can show very good attention and concentration with subsequent memory of those characteristics of Pokemon figures while a parent is often befuddled as to why a child can't remember to take out the trash once a week. Many children are not particularly hyperactive but are diagnosed ADD and prescribed Ritalin because they're doing poorly in school with the hope that Ritalin will improve grade performance. Long-term grade improvement with Ritalin rarely occurs unless the improvement is caused by something unrelated to medicating the child. No drug will develop interest, motivation, perseverance, joy in learning, or other characteristics necessary to do well in school. While some ADD-behaving children's grades go up after the prescription is obtained, a few years down the road, often much sooner, grades do not remain at higher levels.

Tom Sawyer, Huck Finn, Dennis the Menace, Wednesday and Pugsley Adams, and Bart Simpson could have been diagnosed ADD and put on Ritalin. Not that it would have helped any. Were these children brain damaged or genetically preprogrammed, or did they have parent(s) that were absent, ineffective, constantly excusing away their behavior, even finding humor in it, and poor disciplinarians? Their parents seemed helpless to change their misbehavior. I know, because I have met them.

I've found when administering psychological tests to children, even specific neuropsychological tests that assess the capacity for sustained attention, concentration, memory, either visually and auditorially based, children are quite capable of functioning in a normal or non-ADD range on tests.

During one period of time when my preteenage son was acting ADD, I gave him some of the auditory discrimination subtests of the Woodcock-Johnson Cognitive Skills battery, and he proceeded to perform quite poorly. On another day I told him I wanted him to improve his test performance and told him I would give him money and other incentives if he could prove to me that he was far more capable than he had been before. He scored far above his chronological age and at the college level in auditory discrimination ability. I have demonstrated repeatedly over the years with children in the presence of their parents how situation specific and contextual the child's ADD behavior really is. Countless times parents tell me their child cannot pay attention, follow one- or two-step commands, or do anything that requires any sustained attention and concentration. Yet before their very eyes I ask their child to do four or five or six different things in a row in my office to demonstrate their capacity to listen and follow directions. Often that awakens a parent's recognition of psychological causes of their child's defiant or passive resistance to their requests and helps them move away from viewing their child as neurologically incapacitated.

I've found with absolute reliability in every ADD child's psychological test battery obvious psychological factors associated with causing or maintaining ADD behavior. Parental disagreement, anxiety, depression on the child or parent's part, recurring marital conflict or impending separation or divorce, and lack of emotional or psychological (parenting) involvement often appear. I have never come across a child who exhibited ADD behavior on a particular psychological test or task who could not be reinforced, manipulated, or taught to act non-ADD on that very task with relatively little effort or at least eventually. Inconsistent test patterns are often found as a child will perform ADD on one test and non-ADD on a similar test measuring the same skill.

Much of my previous research involved the identification of ADD behavior patterns on psychological tests. Certain test patterns and responses could reliably discriminate between ADD children and non-ADD children. However, the existence of ADD behavior on psychological tests does not confirm that the ADD behavior is caused by something neurological. Look at research articles and try to answer the question, "How do we know if ADD behaving children scored lower on tests due to lack of interest, or effort, or undeveloped perseverance compared to children who had already developed these skills?" The ADD test responses on psychological procedures can be modified by simply changing environmental or psychological conditions. In fact, the psychological tests used to evaluate children support a psychological cause of ADD much more than provide evidence of a neurological processing deficit or dysfunction. True neurological diseases or disorders are much more reliably resistant to psychological changes, improved performance, or environmental demands on tests. Neuropsychological evaluations of children and adults show that when a true neurological problem (seizure, head injury) is apparent in a child, the child's ability to act non-ADD is considerably less. I found through evaluating elderly people with dementia over a 16-year period at a hospital where I consult that getting an elderly demented patient to develop appropriate sustained attention and concentration, or non-ADD behaviors, would be very difficult, no matter what I did or how great the incentive or manipulative technique was. Individuals I've seen in my office in either a prescription drug intoxicated state or nonprescription drug intoxicated state are unable to exhibit non-ADD behavior so easily. The same is true for someone in significant physical pain, or who has peripheral hearing or visual loss or any other condition wherein an obvious medical or neurological problem or deficit exists.

The variability of ADD behavior, school grades going up and down, performance variations in a particular subject from F to A to F again argue against a static "disease" process in a child's brain.

I've worked as a consulting psychologist to a locked juvenile detention facility for many years. Male teenagers are sent to this facility after exhibiting a long history of ADD behaviors and antisocial behavior in particular. Boys stay at least nine months and sometimes longer at this residential facility. Many of them come in with a history of psychiatric or psychological treatment and evaluations. Many come with current prescriptions for psychotropic medication, even with a past history of prescription drug abuse. Many of these boys have been prescribed Ritalin for many years. It is not unusual for the prescribing physician to be unaware of the extent the child abused Ritalin and other medications such as Dexedrine or Adderall. Stimulants are often used and abused concurrent with other drugs. Even if a prescribing physician did not know all of the inappropriate things their ADD patient was doing, one has to wonder how closely they assessed their patient's behavior, or more probably, how often the parent failed to inform the doctor of the child's behavior in totality.

Most significant about this experience was that the program expectations and my consultative efforts were geared toward non-drug treatment approaches. Boys were taken off their prescription medications, not just Ritalin and other stimulants, but antidepressants and anti-anxiety drugs. Some had even been prescribed major tranquilizers and anticonvulsants in combination with these other medications. Any time a boy was left on medication, it was atypical. One example was a boy who was court ordered not to have the psychiatrist's prescription tampered with. Some boys were prescribed a major tranquilizer, and anti-anxiety agent, and a stimulant medication at the same time by parents trying to control their child's behavior prior to coming to the program.

The juvenile detention facility program is highly structured with boys living there 24 hours a day. They go to school there and are engaged in a variety of other therapeutic activities. Feedback on a boy's behavior is available 24 hours a day from staff counselors who interact with the boys one-on-one, and different teachers who have the boys in the classroom during the day, and monitors in the dining room. Their behavior is highly scrutinized. When walking from one activity or building to another, they are asked to walk quietly, hands at their side, almost as if in a military boot camp. Strict behavior during meal times is requested and adhered to. Counselors are in the boys' classroom to induce compliance toward learning and teacher requests. Behavioral expectations during group therapy and other educational teaching times are well defined under various community norms and rules. Feedback and confrontations throughout the day occur in an attempt to provide clarification and adherence to rules and norms. Various consequences involve time out, removal from the community, writing assignments, loss of various privileges, and one-on-one or group process confrontations. In this very structured therapeutic milieu, it is quite obvious to all staff participants that a boy's misbehavior or ADD behavior is highly situational. The boys make choices as to how to behave, and ADD behaviors are situation specific. It becomes quite obvious that a boy's ADD behavior is much more related to choice, defiance, reluctance to do something, lack of interest, self-righteous anger or resentment, and mistaken perceptions of other people being at fault. Willful disobedience and defiance is typically more of a problem than a boy's inability to sustain attention, to lack concentration, to act impulsively, or to remain hyperactive.

These boys grew up in family situations that were relatively nonstructured. They were not taught to develop their own internal psychological capacity to delay gratification, act reflectively, and be more consciously aware of their needs in relationship to others throughout their life. Legal constraint and control that should have been developed early on in life had to be forced upon them through the judicial system. Studies of family structures with these boys revealed considerable inconsistency and psychopathology, including abuse, divorce, lack of rules, no authority figure in the home, inappropriate anger and other emotional responses, and problems that occurred on a day-to-day basis that molded and shaped them to act ADD and rebelliously delinquent. Boys in the program are expected to develop normative behaviors, follow rules, and confront each other when exhibiting inappropriate behavior. Strict control over the boys' behavior is expected and implemented, most likely far more than they had been used to in their families. Academic performance of A's and B's is a requirement and expectation, rather than a boy's performance being excused by labeling it a learning disability. Expectations of non-ADD behavior are implemented, and considerable improvement is shaped. Prior to coming to the program, ADD behavior was much more frequently expressed at home and in school, and not as effectively changed through medication management.

Even the most severely ADD-behaviored boys in the program exhibit times when they're not acting ADD, especially when interested or motivated to change behavior because of situational factors. One boy was administered Tegretol, Ritalin, and Zoloft. He was quite obnoxious and hyperactive, regardless of the amount of medication. He was taken off the medication and eventually became less ADD-behaviored, and in fact was non-ADD most of the time. This was a typical response by other boys on multiple medications. Every boy that was taken off psychotropic medications, stimulants in particular, was found to be non-ADD in most situations, whether it be in a classroom environment, free time during breaks, in group therapy, or any other aspects of the therapeutic milieu. There were no boys who were unable to be non-ADD in a variety of circumstances and exhibit sufficient control over their responses when responded to appropriately.

The nurse at the program stated the following:

> I have been a nurse at a serious habitual offender program for boys ages 13-19 years old for the past five years. Our program is a 24-hour, 7-day-a-week rehabilitation center for juveniles who have repeatedly broken the law.
>
> During intake screenings 7 out of 10 residents inform me that they have taken some kind of medication for hyperactivity in the past. After reviewing available psychiatric records and talking to guardians, I have found that at least half of all the residents entering our program have taken medication for attention deficit disorder or depression. Some were referred to psychiatrists by their public school systems as kindergartners or first graders in order to control their classroom behavior. Most started taking medication in early adolescence when they were defiant and rebellious during classroom situations or when they had their first encounter with the law. Drug abuse usually starts at the same time schools are reporting disruptive classroom behavior. I feel that schools and parents are looking for a psychological diagnosis to explain their child's behavior and a magic pill to fix their child's outbursts which are causing confrontations with authority figures.
>
> After discussing at length a medication history with the resident, I have discovered that they are noncompliant while at home with medication regimes. Residents will admit to multiple drug use, including alcohol, marijuana, and cocaine while taking prescription drugs for ADD or depression. Even with admissions of noncompliance and drug addictions, residents still request medication "to help them get through this program." Residents express that they are fearful they cannot complete a program without medication. I have never found this to be true.
>
> We have treatment team meetings which include myself, case managers, teachers, and staff to discuss

and review residents' behaviors. I then recommend to the psychiatrist to discontinue behavior modification medication so that we may establish a baseline behavior while in a controlled drug-free environment. Medications are discontinued for a 30-day trial period. I cannot recall medication ever being re-prescribed after the trial period ended.

One of our most difficult residents was a 13-year-old who could not sit still during class, talked out of turn, tapped his fingers, or shook his legs continuously. He was annoying and aggravated the other residents and disrupted school whenever possible. This same boy could sit down in the evenings and read an entire book or play a complete game of chess. Our program finally convinced his family and the psychiatrist to discontinue his cocktail of medications (Zoloft, Adderall, and Depakote). Many staff, including myself, were concerned that they now would have even worse behavior to deal with. Much to everyone's surprise this resident's behavior did not worsen when medications were stopped.

Residents at our program have family situations which are sometimes unbelievable. They are rarely raised by their birth parents. Parents are often children themselves. Guardians are often grandparents or aunts. Their home environments are unstable and unstructured. These young men have not lived with rules, curfews, chores, or family obligations. When they become adolescents, they have not learned to delay self-gratification or impose self-control and are often labeled with ADD when in actuality they have adolescent onset oppositional-defiant disorder (ODD), which no medication can cure.

Because of my past experiences with adolescents diagnosed with ADD, I will continue to recommend behavior modification over medication.

Many times parents will be resistive to the idea of taking their child off the medication, so in those cases we document a child's baseline ADD behaviors in a medicated state, to be compared with documented baseline ADD behaviors in a nonmedicated state. Many parents don't realize that the medication has virtually no significant long-term effect on a child's behavior. They believe medication helps.

Often there exists what is termed a placebo effect in a parent's expectation of the "benefits" of stimulant medication. Placebo effects have been discussed in detail in an interesting book by Fisher and Greenberg (1997) entitled *From Placebo to Panacea: Putting Psychiatric Drugs to the Test*. They make a valid point that with ingestion of a prescribed substance believed to have positive effects, there is a sufficient expectancy effect. They argue that most of the "positive" effects of most psychiatric drugs can be attributed to placebo.

I find this particularly true with prescription of antidepressants in patients where they're expecting that they're going to be less depressed. Whether the medication actually makes them happier or not is another issue. Medications provide some physiological reaction, and a subjective interpretation of that reaction is attributed to be positive.

The often heard phrase "a chemical imbalance" is given to justify chemical treatments by some despite no evidence that a "chemical imbalance" exists. Next time someone like your doctor suggests you or your child have a chemical imbalance ask them the following questions: Did you measure my chemicals? How? Which ones? How do you know they are imbalanced? What are the reference criteria—who's chemicals are you comparing mine to? How will you know if my chemicals are back in balance? You say research has shown that others with my problem have a chemical imbalance? Can I see it?

I found in my experience with pediatricians that parents can be enormously unreliable and inaccurate presenters of the overall psychological status of their child's ADD behaviors. It's not unusual for a parent, when providing feedback to the pediatrician, to include statements such as "They're doing fine," or "They're so much better," or "He's doing wonderfully in school," or something positive, when in actuality their child is far from performing in such positive manners. Some of this I believe comes from a parent's desire to see some sort of sedating or restricting change in a child's emotionality or behavior. Because there is some relief in that regard, the stimulant medication is described to be "working." In that sense *something* is described as better than *nothing*. However, when looking more specifically at whether there really was *something* behaviorally improved in the children in this detention facility, there really was nothing of significance that the stimulant medication seemed to be doing when behavior was actually observed or scrutinized more carefully. Through various psychological methods in the structured and therapeutic milieu, staff was able to agree, as were children's parents, that the child's ADD was resolved at least for the duration of the program. Also of related interest were boys prescribed antidepressants before entering the program who were subsequently taken off the antidepressants and eventually showed no recurring evidence of depression.

I might be criticized that I have consciously or unconsciously preselected children I work with in my practice. All I can say to this is that I see people of varying socioeconomic backgrounds, different levels of intellectual and academic success, severe to mild levels of psychopathology, and that I have made a conscious effort for many years to never turn a patient away because they can't afford to see me. I see many people for free or reduced fee, and I do not stop therapy with a patient because their insurance runs out. Parents in my community come from very poor socioeconomic areas to very affluent neighborhoods, from relatively unskilled and manual labor occupations, to higher skilled professional or educational positions.

My case study approach in this book is not the same as a randomly selected treatment group versus a control group treatment design. My results cannot be considered a result of a research experiment. Nevertheless, ADD behavior is quite easily observed in children, and the absence of ADD behavior is also quite easy to observe. I obtain and provide ample observations of the existence or nonexistence of ADD behavior, not just over the short term. I base my findings on long-term follow-up, and long-term or permanent behavior changes. Many so-called experimental research designs are not as valid as they are often presented. Particularly when new research studies show up on TV or professional journals that tend to give the public the impression that because it's "research," it must necessarily be true. A typical lay person does not realize how much a clinical psychologist has studied numerous courses on statistics, experimental research design and analysis, and sometimes conducts their own research without conclusive findings. There is very little conclusive research in the field of medicine and psychology. Many so-called experimental research designs are truly experimental. There are not placebo or control group studies where patients and/or researchers/therapists in clinical studies know to one degree or another who is getting the placebo and who isn't (Fisher and Greenberg 1997).

Most researchers do not account for the effects of a child's being on medication prior to an experimental procedure. Some confuse or avoid the problem of correlation versus causation all together. I have yet to find a stronger research design where the researchers used a procedure as follows: Given a sufficient number of diagnosed ADD and non-ADD children, make sure the ADD child has not taken psychotropic medication just prior to the study. Account for children who have true medical problems. Ask the ADD children to pay attention and motivate them to do well. Ask or train the non-ADD children to act ADD, and measure/scan *their* brains. Provide a third group of children who act "upset," "angry," or "anxious" and assess their brains. Ask all the groups to perform tasks and watch their brain activity. It's most likely that any changes in glucose metabolism or blood flow on scans that ever did show up someday would simply be a function of expressed activity levels in a child, prior drug use, or neurological differences based on learning ADD behavioral approaches to tasks.

There are no adequate long term experimental studies on ADD. One only needs to cite clinical experience showing that psychiatric drugs for children's ADD behavior problems have very little, if any, benefit with regard to specifically eliminating ADD behaviors over the long term. The criterion I use to define an ADD cure include the strength of a teacher's report, parent's report, clinical observation by the therapist, objective psychological tests or measurements provided, change in school grades, and ADD behavior changes that last indefinitely, at least on later follow-up with parents many years later. These are stronger than the typical criterion measures used in most experimental and clinical research designs.

One need only to go into a classroom or into a child's home to monitor an ADD child who is on psychotropic medications to realize that those children still act ADD to one degree or another while in a medicated state. One only needs to demonstrate that an ADD child can pay attention and concentrate on a variety of tasks when sufficient interest and motivational factors are considered. Simply visit a child's home or classroom after a period of successful psychotherapy and observe whether a child is still ADD or not. Most research studies looking into the effects of ADD-behavior treatments do not review long-term psychotherapy, family psychotherapy, or family approaches. Often when drugs are compared to placebo, they are compared with "psychosocial treatments" that are quite different from what I do in my office with children and their families.

What parents need to know is that many mental health practitioners believe or will tell them their child is incurable or at least needs medication. If a referral is made for therapy or counseling, it is not believed or intended by others to be a true cure for their child's ADD. It is my opinion that parents need to be involved in some type of therapeutic or counseling experience geared toward changing the parents primarily, rather than their child being seen individually, or the parents receiving "advice giving" only in their counseling. Otherwise, treatment may be quite limited in its long-term effects on their child because of what I consider misguided beliefs by many in the American psychiatric, medical, and psychological professions. I spent a lot of years earlier in my career practicing the ways many others do, following the same beliefs in some part, only because I was relatively inexperienced. Fortunately, I've always been curious enough about what people do to look beyond the obvious and the superficial verbal presentations of what people say. To me, actions sometimes speak louder than words, and there is always more to it than meets the eye.

9
The Therapeutic Process

It's surprising how many persons go through life without ever recognizing that their feelings toward other people are largely determined by their feelings toward themselves, and if you're not comfortable within yourself, you can't be comfortable with others.

—Sydney J. Harris

I have discovered that all man's unhappiness derives from only one source—not being able to sit quietly in a room.

—Pascal
(1670)

You do not need to leave your room. Remain sitting at your table and listen. Do not even listen, simply wait. Do not even wait, be quite still and solitary. The world will freely offer itself to you to be unmasked, it has no choice, it will roll in ecstasy at your feet.

Franz Kafka

The unexamined life is not worth living.

—Socrates
(circa 470 - 399 B.C.)

I am always ready to learn, although I do not always like being taught.

—Winston Churchill
(1952)

Psychotherapy is the search for the meaning of a parent and child's problems, a meaning that is unknown to them and why there is such underdeveloped motivation to act upon what they should do. A parent's words are what provides access to understanding the meaning. Words provide an inroad into a parent's intentions, beliefs, attitudes, and perceptions, to further elucidate what's behind the ADD behavioral response in a child. Words in therapy are what connect us to what was previously not understood; without them, we are stifled and will remain lost as to why our child will not become non-ADD.

When parents can't speak freely what's on their mind with an uninterrupted, honest, curious intent, it is because there is something blocking that process. Perhaps a parent has not been taught to appreciate the power of one's mindful opinions, or something is too bothersome, scary, or uncomfortable to own up to. When we are stifled in the ability to think and talk freely, we lose the path of understanding and are left vulnerable to the bioreductionistic medical model approaches.

At any given moment in time a parent can choose to think or act, whether it be talking or listening, in a multitude of ways. What should I say next? What should I do next? This human process of thinking, of choosing, or being aware (reflecting) is acting non-ADD. It is a fundamental act of human behavior. We have free will. We go through this choosing process consciously and unconsciously, whether we admit it or not. When we can better understand how we act in ways we don't even realize, we are in better control of ourselves and our children.

To what degree parents are able to choose or determine how they act in the next moment with their ADD-behaving child determines how both parent and child will act in their next moment of thinking or behaving. We can all act differently. Parents experiencing a problem with their child's misbehavior may have become unable to continue this thinking or choice process to produce better behavior with their own child for various reasons. Parents become frustrated, disappointed, hopeless, apathetic, preoccupied, or too overwhelmed to continue thinking about it and discovering the unseen but to-be-discovered causes. When a parent comes to see me looking for answers about how to teach their child how to behave better in a non-ADD way, they have simply been unable to carry forth this choice process in a more effective manner on their own.

Successful psychological treatment of ADD problem behaviors in children has some common elements, no matter which therapist a parent is working with. There is also a lot of individual variation amongst therapists who can provide successful work. It's difficult to come up with a canned therapy approach, but it is important to describe what seem to be common elements of successful therapy.

Common elements necessary in the treatment of ADD behavior problems may involve awareness of what's been discussed thus far and then a thorough examination of all the many beliefs and ideas parents have about themselves, their child, and their life in general. Specific therapeutic techniques must be geared to make parents responsible about talking about their own thoughts and feelings about themselves, their spouse, and their child in particular.

Often there is a direct correlation between the severity of ADD behavior and the parents' willingness or ability to say what's on their mind to a therapist. Generally, but not always, parents who have learned to be more introspective, psychologically-minded, or talk about thoughts and feelings as if these psychological factors have an importance in their day-to-day life, are more inclined to benefit from therapy quicker. They are more acceptive or responsive to the notion that their ADD-behaviored child is not a victim of brain chemical imbalances or genetics. Those parents are more apt to verbalize in a more honest and accurate way how they respond and relate to their ADD-behaviored child.

Parents vary in their ability to say whatever comes to mind. Some are less able. My work with those less able parents involves more talking on my part. Ultimately my verbal and non-verbal responses are generally aimed at eliciting a "free associative process."

All parents have to be taught how to free associate. A lot of experience and patience is required by a therapist to realize that if a parent comes to their office and says *everything* that comes to mind, parents can psychologically figure out themselves and their child. One of the long held beliefs of psychotherapy is the goal to increase someone's knowledge or insight about what causes them to do what they do. Changing perceptions, attitudes, and thoughts is crucial for a psychological change and is part of every successful therapy process to one degree or another.

Psychoanalytic or psychodynamic therapists have often been criticized for their silent, abstinent, or passive response at times to a person's questions or verbal material in therapy sessions. But there is nothing to criticize when a parent finds in therapy that thinking out loud requires their own active participation and paves the way toward self-reflection and knowledge. In fact, the ability to be reflective and free associate is a positive end result. ADD behavior is, by definition, a lack of reflectivity and insightful forethought. Few people can argue that positive change occurs with improved knowledge about change factors. This requires an active psychological process, not a passive process wherein one is expected to be magically cured with simple ingestion of a pill or "given" the answers to their questions.

There are all kinds of variations on how to teach people to free associate, much of them quite familiar to those who tend to practice more from an insight-oriented psychotherapeutic perspective.

If one is willing to look for meaning beyond what is immediately obvious and search for acquisition of new information, in other words to learn, the process is set in positive motion. Sometimes it is very difficult for parents to realize there is an unconscious. The unconscious is defined only as something as yet out of a parent's awareness. *Unconscious* can also be described as what is unknown and information as yet unobtained or knowable.

I try to make it more acceptable to a parent by stating things like, "Well, that's how everybody solves problems in life." To put one's mind to something. To brainstorm, "think tank," let one's mind wander, babble aimlessly, talk impulsively, daydream, mindlessly meander. *Not* to think of what to say but to say what one's thinking. This is no different from the car mechanic who works on my car's engine. I bring symptoms to the car mechanic, and the car mechanic proceeds to look under the hood, tinker about, and search for what he will hopefully eventually find is causing the problem. While the car mechanic's tools are wrenches, a psychologist deals with psychological problems; and their tools are a parent's words, thoughts, attitudes, perceptions, memories, feelings, and so on. What is psychological has to do with feelings, thoughts, attitudes, and behaviors, and all that is psychological is the focus of our scientific inquiry or investigation into a child's developing ADD behavior problems. When someone says everything that comes to their mind, they are verbalizing thoughts, memories, dreams, and things that are psychological, not mechanical or linked to nuts and bolts, which the auto mechanic focuses on. We are becoming psychological detectives searching to find missing pieces of a puzzle. To free associate is to put all the pieces of the puzzle on the table while looking for connections.

It is very difficult for most people to realize that someone could come and sit in my office once a week and say everything that comes to their mind and psychologically be able to change how they think, feel, and act toward their children without me *doing something else*. A parent will sometimes say, "What's talking going to do?" "I already do that," "I talk to myself all the time," or "We always talk." I point out that, while they may do that, what we do is different in some ways. They may get distracted by something else. Something bothersome may come to mind and they don't know where to go next with the thoughts or feelings. They may not realize the different impact saying things out loud to another person may have. Besides, parents *don't* tell somebody else everything, because of what that person may think about their most private thoughts or feelings. We also don't have someone who knows how to help us access new information when we're stuck in our thoughts. Most of us don't take the time to pursue our thoughts toward healthier resolutions. Troublesome thoughts just stay stuck in our minds, and the free associative process frees up our thinking.

Here is an exercise to do for a moment to illustrate what the free associative process involves. Write on a paper or talk into a tape recorder *everything* that comes to your mind. Don't hold back. Put into words everything you are aware of. Memories, feelings, thoughts, what you see, what you hear, etc. When your mind goes "blank" or you are aware you've stopped writing or talking, say or write that. But *don't* stop writing or talking. Do this for 45 60 minutes and you may become interested in what comes out or what comes to your mind. Now do this with another person, and you will find even more comes out about how you think or feel about that person. You may believe it's impossible for you to find out anything new about yourself. If you keep looking for answers and searching for meaningful information, you will find it by not engaging in your usual way of thinking about your problems. We become limited by our own perceptions.

You may think, "What does this have to do with anything—my child or why I came to see you?" That's where the therapist is needed to reassure you that eventually you will make connections to what you find out while engaged in the free associative process. It is very difficult for people to take the time and have patience to reflect upon themselves and their lives in such an intensified manner. We are used to getting what we want very quickly: our food, our mail, our travel, our answers, at increasingly quicker rates in society. Introspective self-reflection is not valued or reinforced enough. Sometimes good things take time. It is inconceivable that the years we've spent acting, thinking, feeling, and developing habits are going to change overnight. Our learning histories are not going to be revealed in one or two therapy visits.

Common misconceptions of the free associative process include the thought that if someone gives me enough information, then I will be able to tell them what caused their child's ADD behavior. I know only general things about parenting and children who act ADD, but not the specifics or particulars unique to every parent who comes into my office. I don't know yet what specific circumstances in that parent's life caused or led up to the parent's inability to teach their child to be non-ADD. It is in this uniqueness and intimate exploration into the psychological life of an ADD-behaviored child and their parents that we find answers. Most parents believe that coming to a psychologist will enable them to learn something new, get some kind of information from the psychologist on how to effect more positive changes in their child's ADD behavior. It is understandable that a parent says, "Tell me what to do," or "Give me the answers."

I have found that a much better way than providing these answers directly to parents is to teach them a way to develop their own answers. I have been able to teach parents to develop their own answers by specifically learning to engage in the thinking and searching process that we all do partially anyway, just to a more psychologically healthy extreme in a controlled therapeutic environment. Parents have to be willing to consider the notion that I can teach them to come up with answers on their own, and usually find theirs are better than mine. Contrary to popular thinking, we psychologists don't sit back and have all the answers; but we're trained to help people find them.

Most people don't realize that solutions are available to them if they trust their own ability to "follow up" their hunches and inclinations and what at first glance seem unrelated or "crazy" ideas. Most of the time, patience on my part and letting them know very clearly that their child will get better (change) will suffice. They do have to say everything that comes to their mind, even though silences are inevitable. There is a tendency to think all we know is what we are aware of or what is conscious to us. We easily forget that life is an ongoing active learning (thinking) process, and we can come to know things that previously we did not know. While this may seem obvious on one hand, it explains in part the frequent response I get from parents who say "I don't know" or "nothing comes to my mind" or "my mind has gone blank." There is certainly an expectation that the psychologist or therapist will give parents the missing information they are seeking, but it comes about in a different way. I'm actually teaching a parent to think reflectively and non-ADD when I ask them to tell me everything that comes to their mind. Most parents don't realize, unless they've already been through psychotherapy, that simply saying everything that comes to one's mind is a mental exercise designed to think more deeply and search out new information.

One father, I remember, insisted that nothing came to his mind and that all he could state was "I don't know." I told him to state "I don't know" as many times as he needed to, to prove that eventually something other than "I don't know" would come to his mind. He thought I was a bit nuts, but complied. After about twenty-five "I don't knows," he smiled and said "Well, there is something else that came to my mind."

Sometimes I will simply nod, smile, remain patient, say "Uh-huh. What do you think?" when a parent is beginning to free associate. Often this process is very difficult for someone to develop. It requires trust, risk taking, a willingness to look into the emotionally unknown, and active energy and motivation on a parent's part. When a parent resists the free associative process and states "my mind is blank" or "I don't know what to say" or "there's nothing on my mind," sometimes I might say, "Well, let's start with telling me what color my walls are. Verbally point out that you are aware of the clock on my wall, and literally say everything that comes to your mind." Usual resistances or comments would involve statements such as, "Well, what does that have to do with anything?" or "I would feel stupid" or "I would feel embarrassed saying that" or something indicating an unwillingness on some level to do what is asked.

Not just ADD-behaving children resist doing what is asked. At this point sometimes it's helpful to redescribe how the free associative process will help a parent change their child's ADD behavior or maybe remind them of something we've already accomplished. For example, I might point out to the resistant parent to remember when we talked about teaching their child to brush their teeth and that was the same problem as teaching a child to sit at their desk in math class and study numbers. When the parent improved their effectiveness in teaching teeth brushing, the child's math improved. This sometimes helps them see connections where there were none before.

What is also intriguing about the free associative process is that since ADD is characterized as impulsiveness as opposed to reflectivity, the very act of engaging parents in saying whatever comes to their mind involves reflectivity and helps parents learn to become more reflective rather than ADD themselves. I've often found that children can accompany their parents to the session and talk quite reflectively about areas of interest or issues that they are attentive to for one reason or another, but when asked to talk about something else they're not particularly interested in such as their math homework, children claim incapacity to reflect upon addition and subtraction. Even when I ask them to talk about numbers and they say they have no thoughts about numbers or no idea what I'm getting at, I tell them, "Well, tell me everything you can that comes to your mind about a number." I can eventually prove to them that they can even think reflectively about numbers and learn to add and subtract and pay attention to how to do those processes.

Much in the field of learning disabilities is based on the notion that a child's brain cannot process certain kinds of verbal, visual, auditory, or tactile input because something neurological causes the child to be unable to do it. There's no doubt in my mind that much of the time spent determining whether a child isn't paying attention because of a hypothetical brain processing problem such as the often heard "central auditory processing disorder" becomes a fruitless search for something that does not exist.

Unfortunately, some testing methods in the field of special education and learning disabilities are often rendered ineffective by this kind of thinking, that a child is incapable of learning because of something that has caused them to be a "victim" or have something missing or less functional than what is in another child's brain. Human beings tend to resort to the simplest and easiest explanation when frustrated with an inability to change behavior. Discussion with any experienced or astute special education teacher will confirm that many of the learning problems a child has in school spring from the family environment or psychosocial factors a child is confronted with and relatively less than with how their brain functions. I am presently amazed how a child can auditorially or visually process information when I tell them I'm going to sufficiently reward them if they take their time and do well on a particular subtest of the Halstead Reitan battery or the Woodcock-Johnson achievement battery tests. Scores on specific tests requiring auditory processing, visual processing, or attention to tasks show considerable improvement and nonimpaired functioning with a child given sufficient motivation to perform. Given sufficient reinforcement, motivation, or interest, many children's learning disabilities could eventually disappear.

Often when parents tell me their children can not do one or two chores because they'll forget them and they lack the capacity to remember or carry out tasks, I immediately demonstrate in my office before their very eyes that their child can remember even five or six different things to do in sequence. This tends to get a parent's attention quite quickly. It goes to the heart of significant long-term controversies within the field of mental health about a child's capabilities. It resonates with the old argument about nature versus nurture and whether the brain is in command of the child's attentional processes and ADD behavior or whether the child and the parents are in command of training the brain to pay attention and act less ADD.

Learning involves focused repetition. Even truly brain-damaged individuals can learn through repetition. The field of cognitive rehabilitation has helped to show that head injured or stroke patients can improve cognitive skills

Often the parent's resistive statement provides an immediate inroad into what should be appropriate objects of analysis in the therapeutic relationship with the parent. I remember one reluctant parent being unwilling to comply with my request. After naming off a variety of objects in my room, they paused and stopped talking. I asked them what happened, and they stated, "Oh nothing." I said, "Well, it appears to me that you started naming off objects in my office and then you stopped, so I'm thinking something probably came to your mind that you didn't want to say." The parent reluctantly became tearful and talked about psychological issues that were eventually quite relevant to why their child acted ADD. Parents have to be taught that talking about a child's brushing their teeth at night in compliance with their request to develop good dental hygiene is very similar psychologically to the parents' request that a child complete their math homework so they can study numbers. Brushing one's teeth and studying numbers both involve an active reflectiveness and obedience rather than impulsiveness.

Once a parent is able to free associate, in other words, say everything that comes to mind, very little on my part needs to be said. An occasional question may come up or I may make a comment. Usually it will have to do with clarifying or supporting the free associative process and explaining how it works.

Therapy takes a lot of patience and nonverbal interest on my part to follow the train of verbalizations (associations), always looking for moments when the verbalizations stop and sometimes simply stating, "What comes to your mind next?"

Generally in my work with ADD families and psychotherapy in general, I try to move parents toward free associating the entire hour. Sometimes I'll talk, chat, tell jokes, or engage in a different type of interaction with parents at the beginning or the end of the hour. But I try very hard to separate that behavior out from the process work of the sessions, which is mom and dad free associating. Remarks during sessions are usually limited to encouraging insightful discussions, awareness of factors associated with their child's ADD behavior, or to explain or teach how free association works. Sometimes reminders to talk are needed. A therapist must genuinely feel care, interest, curiosity, patience, calmness, self-confidence, or anything else positively similar about parents. When I find myself bored, anxious, angry, impatient, or something similarly negative, it's usually because of something in my personal life that's affecting my work. I expect parents to free associate, but I have to create an atmosphere wherein that will take place. There are some families of ADD children who are able to come in and say everything that comes to their mind, while I simply look, listen, and write notes to myself. With others I spend a lot of the time talking, but my talking is still geared toward trying to be reflective, teach free associating, and essentially reinforce my directive that they need to talk on their own and say what's on their mind to eventually find the cures themselves.

I tend to avoid telling parents what to do, like how to spank appropriately, call time out, or respond to specific examples of their child's misbehavior. But this may happen earlier in the therapeutic process until a parent has learned to talk more freely.

If the child is present we have to set the stage for shaping appropriate behavior, so in the office children are expected to sit, talk or act appropriately and demonstrations can occur. More often than not, I will say "What are your thoughts?" or "What do you think you should do?" or "What comes to your mind?"

There is an enormous tendency for parents to state things like, "Well, you're the psychologist, you're supposed to tell me what to do" or "If all I had to do was sit and talk to myself, I could go home and do that in front of a mirror" or "Other psychologists I've seen on TV or talked to give advice" or "I don't have the answers, that's why I came to see you" or "There's nothing on my mind" or "I don't know." There are all kinds of variations on a parent's conscious and unconscious attempts to resist saying everything that comes to their mind. In these situations, it can be difficult to give advice, but I'm reminded of a quote from Henry David Thoreau who said, "There are few men who do not love better to give advice than to give assistance." I've found nothing more effective than teaching people to come up with their own solutions.

While many parents are willing to believe that I can teach them to come up with their own answers, they also need motivation or someone to encourage, support, demand, or guide them through the free associative process. This is especially important when a parent stops actively engaging in saying everything that comes to their mind, and they appear to be stopping the process and not talking. They report "There is nothing left to say" or "The well has run dry" or "There's nothing else on my mind." Almost always some sort of uncomfortable thought or feeling is impinging upon their awareness.

At this point it can be interesting to ask them why they stopped talking. You have to be able to elicit the parents' trust or faith that although the thought or feeling is uncomfortable, not only is it important to talk about but may have a lot to do with their child's ADD behavior, even though the thought or feeling appears irrelevant to them. When I ask someone to simply start opening their mouth and naming off objects in my room, it is often met with their feeling stupid or like they're being asked to do something strange. That feeling of being stupid may be a reflection of their own conscious or unconscious views of being or feeling stupid as a parent, and can be found to show up in many aspects of their behavior in relationship to their child. Insecure, inhibited, fearful, or anxious reactions in a parent or mistrustful thoughts and feelings toward the therapist can have a lot to do with how they relate to their child. These hesitant or uncomfortable reactions will appear subtly and not so subtly in a parent's willingness to free associate. Not thinking out loud or free associating will impede therapeutic progress. It is most often things parents don't say, admit to, acknowledge, or are unaware of that directly cause ADD behavior problems in their child.

This unusual or uncomfortable thing I ask them to do, which is to say *everything* that comes to their mind no matter what, can be a very scary endeavor. So the therapist needs to be familiar with this process and to always look beyond the obvious for more information.

Often parents are afraid of "going crazy" or "losing control" if they say everything that comes to their mind. Often a parent might be afraid of being viewed as stupid, undesirable, unlovable, dumb, incompetent, or have many other negative self-perceptions that make it difficult for them to say everything that comes to their mind. It is often important to develop a therapeutic attitude that nothing a parent tells you is going to be judged or criticized by you, only looked upon as potentially interesting information of assistance to them.

This psychological detective work we engage in has to be conducted with a certain therapeutic attitude of nonblaming and nonjudging. It is an attempt to mutually view their child's behavior with much curiosity and intrigue and a positive expectation of soon-to-be-discovered facts that were previously nonexistent in the parent's mind. There is a constant searching and questioning for what is not immediately obvious. It is a continually expanding and elaborating dialogue or story of their child's behavior. A mystery novel—and in the last chapter we will finally find who or what did it. The creation of faith or trust in the therapist's steadfast knowledge that a parent can teach a child to act non-ADD is crucial.

With parents I am responsible for creating conditions to allow change to take place through their psychotherapy. So determining various motivational factors or reasons for a parent coming to see me is important.

A parent may already know about the limitations of drugging children and agree with you that improved and more effective parenting is what is needed. Yet there are other factors that impede therapeutic progress. Parents come with various preconceptions about what will or will not take place. Some already believe their child is brain-damaged or genetically impaired, and feel their child is not capable of becoming non-ADD in behavior. Some are coming to satisfy the requirement to consult a mental health practitioner because someone told them they had to go, perhaps from a threat that their child may be kicked out of school. Or a parent may get in trouble if they don't comply with someone's demand to see me. Sometimes the parents' prescribing physician told them or encouraged them to see me, and it was mandatory for further prescriptions for medication. Some parents are forced into compliance with legal requirements in a custody dispute, and they are trying to prove that the child needs or does not need medication. Perhaps a parent is seeking help for problems that are not necessarily ADD behaviors but instead are defiance, oppositionalism, depression, withdrawal, drug use, or any number of possible psychological problems in children.

Often a child that comes to my office doesn't exhibit difficulty with hyperactivity and can pay attention and concentrate as well as any other child. But the child is not doing homework or getting good grades in school and resists demands to perform.

In actuality, it is the exception to see a child older than four or five who spends most of his or her time engaging in ADD behavior when a child's behavior is observed during a 24-hour day in its entirety. In other words, no child is in constant motion one hundred percent of the time. Of course, I usually hear the child can "never sit still" or "is always moving" or the child "can not sit still." What I hear typically is not a completely accurate picture of the frequency with which a child actually behaves ADD. Successful therapists understand this fact about children and their behavior.

When parents become more discriminating about the situation, context, and specific behavior on their part that seems associated with the increased likelihood of ADD behavior being exhibited versus the decreased likelihood of ADD behavior being exhibited, they are on their way. In this way one can begin to engage a parent's interest in realizing that behavior is highly situational, and potentially different causes or variables may control their child's ADD behavior. This is important in developing increased awareness on a parent's part. They can learn to have more control than previously thought. Parents have to realize the possibility that if a child behaves differently, it is related to the parents' behavioral response, mood, or time of day.

I'm continually intrigued by the many ways parents view free association as producing thoughts, feelings, or memories they are convinced have nothing at all to do with why they're at my office. Yet most of the time they have everything to do with why the parents come to see me. When a parent comes to see me and I engage them in the free associative process by resisting attempts to tell them what to do, they become uncomfortable through their anxious need to know the answer immediately, and for other reasons. This allows access to unconscious thoughts and feelings previously avoided or ignored by them. Instead I ask them to be patient. These anxious moments of silence and how well the therapist can encourage further free association will determine whether therapy proceeds. It is a fine line we walk, on one hand to blame a parent and hold them responsible for their child's ADD behavior, and on the other, not make them so defensive they quit. At the same time I have to instill hope, confidence, and optimism from their perspective that I'm a supportive therapist who is going to teach them and guide them through the process of learning to become smarter about their child's behavior. One must be able to engage parents in mental aerobics, attend psychology school, and confess their sins all at the same time. Parents need to know they are not perfect people who are expected to do everything right by their child, but they can be held responsible to learn how to teach non-ADD behavior in their children.

Parents are often depressed to some degree or another, partially related to their child's misbehavior and for other reasons. A depressed parent comes to my office seeking help for their unhappiness. They've not found it with Prozac or other psychiatric drugs, which have only numbed their view of their depression or left them feeling differently but not necessarily happy. A depressed person is depressed for various reasons, and one in particular. They have ceased to be able to engage in the free associative process sufficiently to allow them to develop new insight as to why they are so unhappy and depressed. When a depressed parent comes to my office and free associates, eventually tears may come forth, even while medicated. The depression comes back, and they say things like, "Talking about this just makes me more depressed."

It is obvious at those times they have never been chemically reorganized or cured of their depression. If someone has a thought, a memory, or something that comes to their mind that brings back the same depression that they were trying to medicate away, it must still be "lurking somewhere in their mind," so to speak.

Aldous Huxley said in 1946, "If most of us remain ignorant of ourselves, it is because self-knowledge is painful and we prefer the pleasure of illusion." Prescription drugs do little to develop this therapy process of becoming more aware of oneself. Drugs do not help us become creative, spontaneous thinkers, or insightfully and painfully aware of our problems. They cease to motivate us to continue to dig deeper, to think more about something, to even be aware that there is a problem. When a child is medicated, the problem becomes out of sight, out of mind. Rather than medicate a child's ADD behavior I want a child's ADD behavior to cause so much discomfort in a parent they are forced to come see me and talk about how to learn to change that child's behavior. If it didn't hurt or bother us, how would we be compelled to change?

Drugs reduce motivation to search out more difficult but better solutions. They are the "quick fix." When a physician prescribes drugs, it lessens motivation by deadening or desensitizing pain. Personal communications with many physicians over the years reveals a feeling that they "have to do *something* to help these (ADD) kids." Yet the reality is that most parents don't follow-up or receive any kind of counseling or therapy for themselves. Physicians are very reluctant to stop prescribing drugs to their child patients if mom or dad doesn't seek counseling or therapy. Parents often tell the prescribing physician the child is doing so much better on Ritalin, and this lulls the physician into a false sense of security. It is rare for a physician to stop seeing a patient because the parents didn't seek counseling or therapy help, and often parents will not follow through.

When I engage a depressed person in the free associative process, I give them a sense of hope. They had lost hope that there is a cure for their unhappiness. Instead they have been told that they have been victimized by brain damage or genetic abnormalities, just like the ADD-behaviored child. The ADD parent as well as the depressed parent comes to see me, and I tell them, yes, there *is* a cure. They need to believe they can be cured, become happier, and teach their child to be non-ADD. Therein exists a most compelling motive to come back and talk to me. Is it possible that my therapist knows something I don't know about happiness or about teaching a child to act non-ADD?

Clinicians and researchers are limited by the view that temperament and personality characteristics are inborn or genetically developed, and have been unable to learn or benefit from these types of therapeutic experiences. People get stuck in feeling victimized and have lost the ability to realize that the human mind's potential is enormous. Very respectable, intelligent, and caring human beings have tried to help parents solve the ADD problem, but have not gone far enough. Many well intentioned colleagues intuitively know that Ritalin is not the answer. They have not been taught the power of insight-oriented or interpersonal psychotherapy to change children's behavior by working with parents. Often professionals have neither been in psychotherapy themselves nor realize that other therapists can and do cure ADD behavior problems in children. Unfortunately, psychoanalysis, psychotherapy, and "talk therapies" have often been disregarded or viewed as ineffective.

I recently read an interesting paper by Andrew Morrell (1998) entitled "Attention Deficit Disorder and Its Relationship to Narcissistic Pathology." He describes the free associative process in his work with ADD behavior problem children. He states the following interesting perspective on how therapy can be helpful or unhelpful with ADD problems.

> At the broadest level, the burgeoning use of ADD as a diagnosis reflects a cultural trend that is both generally anti-intellectual and specifically anti-psychoanalytic. What is at stake is the role assigned to emotion in the contemporary common-sense theory of behavior and the value attributed to fully experiencing and tolerating all one's feelings, both good and bad. For psychoanalysts, feelings are the core of subjectivity and the royal road to self-knowledge. Therefore, the goal of treatment is to enable people to experience their full range of feelings without needing to either act on them immediately or deny them via defensive security operations. It is believed that if people can tolerate their feelings, then they can use the information that the feelings provide them in order to make life

> decisions that are in their enlightened self-interest. Stated another way, only by fully knowing one's feelings can one determine when and to what degree it is appropriate to act on them. Furthermore, since affect is the language of relationship, it is ultimately desirable, even necessary, to be able to experience the full range of feelings in the service of making intimacy and mutuality possible between people. By contrast, in the minds of the more aggressive bio-behaviorists, feelings are viewed primarily as potential disrupters of smooth functioning and adaptation to the social grid. The goal is to truncate the range of feelings experienced (with a strong emphasis on accentuating the positive) and to train people to behave appropriately in spite of or regardless of their feelings in the hope that if new behaviors are established then feelings will change in accord with them. The emphasis is on result rather than process and on avoidance of interpersonal stress and conflict rather than on "muddling through" to intimacy. Self- knowledge itself, and the introspection and empathy which further it, is minimized in value; what matters is "getting along" with others and not suffering too much internal *sturm and drang*. Medication, in its ability to smooth rough edges and mute strong and upsetting thoughts, feelings, and impulses, is clearly the treatment of choice; analytically-oriented therapy can only stir the waters to no immediately observable avail.

All children will exhibit ADD behavior throughout their lifetime. All we are doing is making them less ADD-behaviored to the point that predictable stable ways of behaving that cause problems for them in their life can be changed. Criteria for curing ADD-behaviored children in this book were observable goals such as A or B school grades in mainstream or regular classes, less misbehavior to the point that parents, teachers, and myself would describe a child as non-ADD or at least "normally" (if not better than normally) behaved, elimination of prescription drugs, and there were no further behavior problems that existed at the start of treatment.

Anyone could engage in psychotherapy or the free associative process for the rest of their life and continue to find problems of thoughts, feelings, or behaviors that they can solve or that can be changed to something more healthy and satisfying. There is no perfectly behaved child, but behavior problems can be specifically defined and specifically changed or cured. When a parent comes to see me, I ask them to be very specific about what they want to see happen with therapy so we know when our goals will be met. Any behavior listed in the *DSM-IV* diagnostic criteria for attention deficit disorder (APA 1994) can be resolved. Any ADD- behaviored child, assuming they are not mentally retarded or have other types of medical problems, can be taught to get A's, and B's in school. All children mentally retarded, with cerebral palsy, seizure-disordered, and head-injured can be taught to act more politely, calmly, cooperatively, reflectively, and focused as long as the problems are specifically defined. A child's personality is an accumulation of various developed situation-specific thoughts and feelings, any one of which can be potentially changed at any time.

It is important to point out that changing a child's ADD behaviors can vary, depending on what the causes of the child's ADD behaviors are. Some families are more motivated, psychologically capable, or skilled, or the cause of the ADD is related to more recent or acute environmental factors or stressors. They require less therapy time. There are other children whose ADD behavior patterns are long in developing over many years and have been developed since toddlerhood.

There are many psychological factors that contribute to the cause of ADD behavior, and often the length of therapy is simply related to the severity of the ADD behavior in a child. Some children come from such psychologically dysfunctional families that years of parenting and family counseling may be required, and sometimes individual therapy with one or both of the parents. In some families the parent's inability to be consistent, organized, and respond to a child on even the simplest tasks makes teaching non-ADD behavior very difficult and trying.

In my experience, successful treatment of ADD behavior problems often takes longer than most parents, insurance companies, or school personnel would like. The insurance industry, particularly managed care, can be a drawback to some parents who seek therapy. Parents need to realize that weekly psychotherapy for many months, maybe even a year or two, is going to take place, and the parent is going to have to reprioritize what they do, sometimes with great resistance. I've often been interested in how parents will spend many hours a week doing all kinds of psychologically unhealthy and unnecessary things, yet to spend one hour in a therapist's office once a week seems so undesirable. Sometimes it's really just a matter of priorities. It's not unusual for me to describe to parents that there are very few things in life that are more important than remolding and shaping a child's psychological character.

A common type of resistance occurs when parents have a hard time taking their child out of school to see a psychologist. Ironically, the hours and hours spent on of ineffective approaches to solving the ADD problem have been in the hundreds over many years. Usually the child's school career is threatened if the ADD behavior problem is not resolved, and missing an hour of school a week is relatively meaningless when the potential gains of therapy are discussed.

One of the goals of successful ADD treatment is to improve a child's academic functioning far beyond what other procedures have gained in the past, whether it be special education classes or psychotropic medication prescription. A child who is unable to learn to pay attention, respond reflectively rather than impulsively, or act calmly rather than impatiently, nervously, or hyperactively, is less likely to learn many things and may develop all kinds of other problems the rest of their life. One smokes, eats too much, gets into trouble, feels unhappy, and has trouble keeping jobs and relationships when one lacks the ability to act non-ADD. Some researchers have studied the long-term effects of ADD behavior and unsuccessful treatment causes alcohol and drug abuse, delinquency, and lack of academic or vocational advancement later in life.

10

One Parent's Experience of Therapy

Five years ago my life took a turn that would put me heading in a different direction. I was 29 years old, married, and had two children, a son and a daughter. Chris was in first grade, and Emma was still at home with me. I started to get notes home telling me Chris was struggling in school. I got deficient papers home telling me he was failing subjects. This went on for a while, and my husband and I tried many different approaches at home to try and help. We could not understand why Chris was failing.

After several conferences at the school, ADD was mentioned. I had heard of it but had not really paid it much attention. I was however, desperate to solve my child's problems. The growing concern I had for him was causing me to feel sick inside. I felt a gnawing inside that I was failing my son, and I wanted to fix the problem and make it go away. That is why I probably jumped at the idea of Ritalin, a wonder drug that would fix my child and make me feel a whole lot better about my child all in two daily doses. How great! He went on the drug, and I felt a lot better. For a while anyway. Of course, then there was the problem that I was still struggling with my own life and its stresses, so I thought that I may have ADD. I had been told it was genetic in nature, so I asked if I might be suffering from this chemical imbalance. Sounded like the solution to my problems. However, my son's doctor referred me to another doctor.

After making an appointment with him, I was told that the problem could be approached from a nonmedical standpoint. I listened. At this point I was open to suggestions. Always a good place to be! Open, that is! Well, he said to come back and talk to him once a week. I said OK, thinking that this man seemed to sound so sure of what he said, although how talking to him for one session a week could possibly fix anything was completely beyond me. However, as I mentioned, I was wide open for suggestions, and this seemed to be the one that was presenting itself at this time. I have to assure you that although I went along with his suggestion to sit for fifty minutes a week and just tell him everything that came into my head, I thought he was the one that maybe had a problem. If he thought that just talking could make my son stop failing school and help me in the chaos that was called my life, I felt for sure he had to be nuts.

Let me tell you something of my life at that point. As I have mentioned, my son was failing school. I had returned to school after being home for eight years and was finding the stress of keeping a home running with two children and being in school extremely stressful. I had been used to stress, though, for all my life. I had been brought up in your typically dysfunctional family with maybe more than the average trauma one has in life. I just think mine was all packed into the early years. I learned life's harder lessons very early. I learned what abandonment felt like at my birth, and I carried on learning the giants in life like rejection and never being good enough. Of course, I carried all this through to my adult years, but told myself that none of it would affect me. I basically became a people-pleasing person who gave my right to happiness away because I did not believe I even deserved it. I spoke no truth. I told people what they wanted to hear so they would not get rid of me. Of course, when I became too enraged that I did not have any right to say what I thought or felt, I would pull away and ended up feeling abandoned anyway, which was the very thing I was trying to avoid. However, these are the things that I know now. Back during the time when Chris was diagnosed with ADD, my life was basically one of survival with a backdrop of intermittent misery. You can imagine why I thought that talking would probably not fix my problems or Chris's. Let me say, though, at the time Chris was diagnosed, although I knew deep inside of me I was not happy, I thought Chris had the problem. At the time I was relieved someone was not pointing their fingers at me.

How things change! I spent the time that was asked of me. I sat and I struggled with therapy. At times it felt like all I did was struggle, but I now see that my struggle was not with therapy—it was with me opening up my eyes and being honest about me. I was so keen to go through life and not get busted. Therapy busts you wide open. While there were parents out there giving their children medications for their problems or medicating themselves for depression, I was sitting down with someone and learning to ask to have my eyes opened. I did not even realize at the time that this is what I was asking for. I just sat and said all the things that I was aware of at that moment. What came forth was often painful and usually messy, but there was always something to be learned. It is not the easy path. Taking pills is easier. So, if you are reading this and you want an easy way out, let me tell you that this is not one. This is some of the hardest work I have ever done in my life. I have often had to summon up more courage to face the truth within me than I have ever had to summon up to face anything on the outside of me. You may be reading this and saying, well, there is nothing about me that I do not already know. I said that. I said that a lot. I thought I knew all there was to know. Let me try and say this gently. You are wrong! There are things about you that you have no idea about. Just ask a friend. An honest one, that is. Ask a friend to tell you something that you do that he or she may see as a concern. More than likely they will tell you something you do not see in yourself. We tend to be blind to our own things.

I have been on a journey into truth about myself. Others have been taking medication. Often those taking medication will say there is no problem. It is genetic for them. I challenge you to think differently. We have so many emotions and thoughts within, and often when the negative ones come up we want to get rid of them. We want to take something that will make them go away. Have you ever thought that this just may be an early warning device? If your warning light goes on in your car, do you just hit it or unplug it so you won't see it? If you do, it does not make the problem that is occurring in the car go away. Your awareness of it may be temporarily gone but, trust me, the problem is still there, and at some point it will cause a major problem. Could we maybe see our own problems in ourselves or our children as a warning that something may be out of whack? Don't drug it out of awareness. Look at it and explore it. Find out what the warning is about. This will take some of that courageous work I was telling you about. But this is life. We are given life to learn about ourselves and grow. In each lesson, painful or joyful, is something to be mastered. If when the lesson comes, you knock it over the head with your choice of drug, whether it be medication, alcohol, food, or the various other options, you choose not to take the lesson and not to grow. The God who made the universe will not support this act.

I have learned many lessons on my journey, and I am still learning. Many of them I journaled as I was living through them.

It is an option other than medication. It is an option of growth. It is a choice to be honest with yourself. It is a choice to look within and to see, really see, what is there. It is a choice to find yourself and where you came from and who you really are. I took that choice and it changed my life. I am still changing. See where I came from and look at my journey. Then make a choice to take a path of drugging yourself out of awareness or bringing yourself into the awareness of who you really are.

Whenever I read or hear about ADD, I do so with a special interest, for although I look at the subject from a nonprofessional viewpoint, I have a very involved position in this issue. I am the parent of a child who was diagnosed with ADD and placed on Ritalin; however, as a family we have now resolved the problem without Ritalin. Most of the information that I have read is from the professional community, and I feel that more should be heard from the parents who are or have been caught up in this issue that is affecting so many families. All views are important, yet I feel that a vital area may be missing from the discussion on ADD. That area is what it feels like to know that so many people do not fully understand what impact one human being can have on another. I do not think people realize the tremendous impact that one person can have on another person's life. I know that when I became a mother, I wanted to give my children everything that I did not have. I knew in my heart that everything was not right with me. I knew that my emotions and behaviors were often out of my control, but I was sure I could cover all this up and be a good parent. I wanted so much in my heart to be a real mother to my children. I read every book I could get my hands on and watched other mothers so I could learn how to care properly for my son. I never intended to be a setback for my child. All I wanted was for him to know what it was like to have a happy childhood.

So, when I hear parents talk about a child's ADD problems and they seem to write it off to every source apart from themselves, I cannot help but smile; but I also feel hurt and frustrated because they do not seem to be looking at themselves to be the solution for their child's problems. I was considered to be a good person and a responsible parent by most of the people I know. However, when my son started to have problems in school, I was faced with a problem and was not sure how to solve it. I was drawn down the avenue of Ritalin. I was told by many that the problem was with my son, and medication would solve the issue. I was wrong. My son took Ritalin for a few months, but something deep inside me was not comfortable with the situation. I acted on this feeling and learned that my problem arose from the notion that I thought I knew everything there is to know about loving children. As I stated, I had every desire and wish to love my children, and I did in the capacity that I had; but I have learned that I did not know enough about myself to be able to do a good job. I knew that my son's problem might be directly related to my own issues, but I had managed by hiding them for so many years. I thought they had remained from view to the world; however, now I can see clearly how so many unresolved issues in my own life affected his development. I cannot help but wonder how many other children diagnosed with ADD have parents with issues that need to be solved. I cannot be the exception, which is why I find it difficult when I hear parents not looking at themselves. Do they look at someone like me and think that I must be different somehow and that is why my son was diagnosed with ADD, or do they think that suddenly children are born this way? Neither of these is true.

I am just an ordinary parent who wants the best for her children, and our children have more potential than we give them credit for. We make our children much of what they are, and much of the time it is not intentional. I never wanted to withhold love from my children. I wanted to be able to have my own son touch me without it causing a bad reaction, and I managed as best as I could, not even knowing why I felt the way I did. When I think of the label ADD that was given to my son, I could think of a much better name for what my son had—"a mother that was too scared to love because of how it made me feel." Is that in the medical books? Can I take a pill to cure it? I probably could. Well, just to cover it up anyway.

One day I would like to sit down with an advocate of Ritalin and the "genetic-factor" and point out some real reasons why a child can have problems. People were so quick to diagnose my son with ADD because they could not see anything externally that could cause his problems. It is funny looking back at myself during that time. The school psychologist saw me as a calm, respectable mother who was concerned about her son, which I was, but this person had no idea about the inner turmoil that I felt. Do people really think we wear big signs on our heads with the issues that we have? I think most people do a pretty good job of hiding them. We are taught to do that. So, of course, people think that because they have hidden their flaws from the rest of the world, we can hide them from our children. This does not happen. Our children receive us in all our forms and are often exposed to parts of us that no one else experiences. Is this possibly one reason why we have growing numbers of children labeled with the diagnosis of ADD? Are they literally taking the rap for what the adults in their lives refuse to confront? It is not my place to judge, but it is maybe time for people to honestly look within themselves and ask searching questions about their own lives and the effect they could be having on others. It is not an easy task or even pleasant sometimes, but the rewards are worth the work because this is the gift of life, our own and others, and it is in our hands to make it work.

A few years go I would and did not want to confront many unpleasant things about myself. In fact, I often now do not want to, but I do know that once you look in those dark places that you are trying to hide from but never seem to fully escape, things start to change. I never thought I would tell another soul some of the thoughts that I had, but I soon began to learn that it was this very openness that made the fear go away. Each problem that I had with my son was traced back to problems in my life. I do not find that easy to say, but it is the truth. It is also an awesome responsibility to know that our behavior can affect another person so much. It is also a great blessing to know that we can influence those around us in a healthy way. It is also a wake-up call for us to take responsibility for our own lives, so we can be a positive influence to others.

I suppose now, looking back, it should have been obvious that, because the only physical touching that I had as a child was sexual and by a male, I associated any physical contact with sexual arousal. I would often avoid skin contact because of how lousy it made me feel. This clearly caused difficulties in my marriage and with my children. I thought that I had hidden the previous trauma well, but these things come out. When my daughter was born, I noticed the difference. I did not feel the same horrible feelings when she would touch my skin. I think this was when I knew that something was wrong. I had always felt that things did not feel completely right, but it wasn't until I had anything else to go on that I was sure. I didn't feel I could go to anyone with this, so I just carried on the best I could. There were many other areas where I had problems, and there still are some things that are not right. But according to many, Chris just had ADD. Each person has his or her own darkness that is particular to them. If people take the time to love and care about each other, maybe people might be honest enough to look at their own darkness and, with the help of caring people, resolve it. But if an easy option is given, it is too often taken. I took that option for awhile until someone showed me the light. We need as many people in the world as possible with a different message than medication and helplessness. If more people were shown an alternative to medication, children would be able to stop wearing the label for someone else's issues. I carried around the blame and burden of my parent's issues, but I will not let my children do that. Soon we will be able to just look at the children to see the problems in society, because they are the ones that many are making take the rap for grown-up problems.

For parents who have a child on Ritalin, I would love to have the courage to ask them to honestly look at their own lives and really spend time contemplating whether there are areas in their lives that could be influencing the problem. I believe that each person has the capacity to know truth; and I feel that if each parent was totally honest, most would come back knowing that there are parental influences that could contribute to the child's problem. The problem is that we are too scared to be honest. I do not know why covering things up seems so much more natural than being honest. I do know that I never chose to have the issues I had in my life, which is why sometimes I get so upset and bitter that I have to be the one resolving them. But when you really think about it, I am sure each person that negatively influences a person's life probably does not want it to happen. I guess you either stay bitter and leave it to someone else, or resolve it so you do not pass it on down the line. It's like passing the buck. I think many know that something has to change, but I suppose it is a matter of who will say that this is enough and take things into their own hands and change situations. But, of course, I was always told that you cannot change who you are. We even have sayings for it: "A leopard cannot change its spots."

God created us in His own image, so why do so many people believe that we go wrong so easily and that most of our problems are genetic? I suppose they must think that there is something wrong with God's creation. We need to understand that we are the ones who are getting it wrong! We are created just fine, and with the right loving we will turn out fine. I know none of us will get it perfectly, but we have the right guidance to go by, which is clearly laid out in God's word and practiced by many believers, and it works. I am amazed at my own ignorance at times, to think that the God who created us would not know what is best for us. With most material possessions, we consult a handbook or manual to learn how to best use the item. We know that the best person to ask about the working and functioning of something is the person who made it. Why then don't we think that God would know what is best for His creation? He knew from the beginning what was best for us. Even when we make mistakes and go the wrong way, He knows how to lead us back to the light. Our responsibility is to look inside ourselves and allow ourselves to be guided by truth. God's primary concern is for the family. He emphasizes the parents' responsibility to instill values and truths in children to create the inner foundation they need in life, yet we do not put enough emphasis in these areas. I was at the check out at Wal-Mart today, and almost every front cover if the magazines said something about the body and beauty and how to improve everything that was external. But what about the inside? Why do we not feed our souls? If every child on Ritalin had more attention given to their emotional and spiritual growth, I wonder how many would still need the medicine. But first the parents have to recognize this need in themselves. Instead of turning to reasons and solutions outside of ourselves, maybe we should look internally for our answers, because they are there, and they work.

11

Bobby—Severe ADD

Bobby first came to see me at the age of six. He was having considerable difficulty in kindergarten. His difficulties ranged from not listening in school and putting plastic bags over his head in class to being extremely disobedient and constantly provoking others. He was impulsive, inattentive, and did not stay on task. He'd often state that he hated someone or that no one liked him. He stole and lied. He was aggressive with small animals and small children.

Bobby's school teacher sent a letter home stating he made animal noises and had to be constantly corrected. He would wander around when he had work to complete. When Bobby was told to sit down, he asked why she was such a grouch. He continually got out of his seat or scooted up and down in his seat after being told to sit in one place. He asked to use the bathroom more frequently than necessary. He shouted out answers, even after being reprimanded. He went to an adjacent classroom, looked in, and yelled in a classmate's ear. He yelled at a coach across the cafeteria. He played with food. This was all in one day, a typical day for him. Another day he was depicted as "running around in the hall acting like an airplane, being unable to sit appropriately in class, distracted and pretty much a handful." Teachers were complaining that he couldn't sit still because of nervousness, was failing subjects, and was being sent to the principal's office frequently.

A behavior problems checklist revealed problems involving lack of self-confidence, moodiness, speaking of himself as stupid or dumb, and often asking if he was loved. He had nightmares, was overly preoccupied with sex, and wandered around aimlessly. He was being rejected by other kids, had no close friend, and exhibited bossiness and the need to be the center of attention. He displayed disobedience toward parents (for which spankings were ineffective), average intelligence, difficulty cutting things with scissors as well as problems with other fine and gross motor skills, periods of seemingly being unaware of what's going on around him, staring spells, delays in self-help skills like dressing and eating, distractibility, impatience, inattentiveness, and an inability to take a nap. Five minutes or less was all he could sit at one time. In talking he would jump from one topic to another, parroting in his speech. He had physical complaints of being too hot or too cold, headaches, episodes of appearing "paralyzed," and having a higher pain tolerance. Bobby seemed unhappy and threatened to run away. His most recent baby-sitter had to quit because of the names he called her. Arguments about who was boss occurred at home and some parental disagreements on child rearing were evident.

Physical and neurological examinations revealed nothing of significance except some "soft neurological signs." Past medical history revealed no significant problems evident when looking at pre- and perinatal birth conditions or developmental milestones. No significant family medical history was obtained, except the father was described as "probably ADD." Bobby's biological mother was 26, working as a secretary, with two years of college education. His stepfather was 27 and worked as a trucker, also with two years of college education. Both parents denied any particular family or marital problems.

Bobby's mother came with him for the initial evaluation. He was referred to me by a pediatrician who is typically very thorough in his work-up of children and quite psychologically minded about them. His mother stated she thought it was "typical kindergarten behavior" at first. In the daily notes about his behavior, the school told her she needed to seek consultation. She had told the principal that they (the parents) had a handle on his behavior at home, and they didn't know why he was having trouble in school. They "decided they would make the school happy" and "get him tested." So that's why they came to see me. Mom and Dad were both angry at the school for being forced into treatment, and there was disagreement about Bobby's need for treatment and whether he was ADD or not. Mom stated she thought the teacher was biased because the teacher's son was ADD. Bobby's parents felt the school just couldn't handle him. They claimed he sat stiff at home and did his homework, although his mother did say that he had problems listening and she would tell him to do things three or four times and he still wouldn't do them. His mother figured he was just bored because the teacher didn't keep his attention. She said she was thinking "it really wasn't a problem, the teacher was just biased and incompetent." She questioned whether he was a typical six-year-old or not. She stated, "We're just doing this to prove there is nothing wrong with him. We told them if there's something wrong with him we'll get him tested." She said she'd seen "other six-year-olds acting this way" and she's done "enough baby-sitting to see there's all kinds of problems out there." Then she stated, "He's just an active child." His mother further stated, "To me this is the way he's always been. He's always been active and gone from task to task. It's never really changed." The school threatened to have him suspended if his parents didn't get help.

The school psychologist evaluated Bobby and stated he had a learning disability described as a central auditory processing disorder (CAP). CAP is a popular attempt amongst some in the school system to describe a child's inability to pay attention as being caused by a hypothetical neurological problem. It is described as central because there is no peripheral hearing loss, which means it must be somewhere in the "center" of the brain and probably "central" to a neurological explanation for his learning (hearing problems). Bobby had a "seizure" three months after beginning Ritalin. He was referred to a neurologist by his pediatrician within the first year of treatment because of the mother's concern about Bobby' s staring spells and "seizures." The neurological evaluation showed a possible partial-complex seizure and possible paresthesias, but eventually nothing neurological was found on head CT, MRI, EEG, or comprehensive physical examination. The neurologist put Bobby on Tegretol in addition to Ritalin and told Bobby's mother that he had a questionable EEG. Bobby took Tegretol for about a year and a half, justified by the supposed underlying neurological problem. The fact that Bobby had tics further implied a neurological cause. After therapy with me involving his mother in a discussion of the obvious secondary gain from his "seizures" and "tics," his tics were resolved and never returned, even after no longer taking Ritalin or Tegretol.

In the initial evaluation the mother revealed that Bobby had a vivid imagination and complained of headaches and nightmares. She said he did get headaches, but she got headaches, too; it was just hereditary. She said the pediatrician sent them to see if "he was OK up here in the head." He told his mother once he was an alien.

He would hit himself or bite himself. She said he got depressed or would sometimes run and run and run. She complained he took her back massager for sexual stimulation. She mentioned he didn't know it yet, but her husband had adopted him when he was two and they had been investigated once for child abuse. Bobby would hyperventilate and get panicky. She went on to say he would "smell things" and have panic attacks over them and call them "hexes." He would say, "It's just the bad air," and the smell was the hex.

During the first interview I observed Bobby to be one of the most hyperactive and non-compliant children who had ever been to my office. He would play with the toys on my desk even though he was told by his mother and me to stop. He would not make eye contact. He would climb on top of my chair and spin around without stopping. He almost pulled down my bookshelf. He repeatedly refused to listen to his mother at all, and would initially comply with my requests, but eventually went back to doing what he previously was doing after a few seconds delay. He was in constant motion, almost "pinging" from object to object. It was obvious his mother had very little control over him and set very few limits.

Later in his treatment with me, Bobby's mother would describe his frequent "panic attacks" or "seizures," words used interchangeably by her, and eventually brought the seizure issue into focus in one session. Bobby came in looking quiet and subdued, but neurologically intact in his appearance and overt behavior, gross and fine motor movements, and cognition. His mother proceeded to describe how worried she was. Perhaps they needed to rethink his medication and take him to the neurologist for a follow-up evaluation. After asking Bobby and his mother to describe the situation in more detail, it became quite apparent Bobby's "seizure" was clearly an attention-getting device, a manipulative attempt to get out of punishment for something he did wrong, and was something he often used to diffuse the threat of punishment. In fact, that week Bobby's parents were having an especially tumultuous time in their marriage, and there was talk of divorce. Finally Bobby stated he was upset about his parents' fighting. He talked about being worried they might get a divorce and talked about the big fight they had that week. He became tearful. Previously he had not expressed depressed mood or affect. His mother brought up how he had talked about having "funny smells" that day, further raising the issue of a true seizure. Since that time there has never been an episode or complaint of a seizure or a panic attack.

A few months later the parents decided to discontinue the Tegretol after consultation with their pediatrician, because they could see no obvious change or improvement with the medication. They discontinued the use of Ritalin about one year into the treatment, because they found no obvious positive effect even though the dosage had been increased to 20 milligrams a day. They complained, "He isn't himself," referring to being sedated and having "the zombie effect." As is the case with any child I've seen on Ritalin, the ADD behavior problems never completely abate even while the child is in a medicated state.

It is often the case that the symptoms parents ascribe to the child are also symptoms exhibited by a parent, which are sometimes admitted to and acknowledged by a parent and sometimes not. Any ADD-behavior child has parents who also exhibit significant ADD behavior, one way or another. I now ask them to tell me about their own ADD in attempt to further insightful thought about the link, between their behavior and their child's. Subsequent discussions of Bobby's "panic" and "seizures" revealed new knowledge on mother's part. She, unquestionably, in her mind had "seizures" described as "panic attacks" in the past. She no longer experienced them after about six months into the therapy process.

Mother's psychological problems were meaningfully related. At the time she entered therapy, she had been clinically depressed for many years. She felt very insecure and would be described by psychologists as having a dependent personality style. She felt very alone, disconnected from her husband, and marital problems were frequently evident. She felt so overwhelmed at times, she later admitted, that she would just give up on "discipline" and control of Bobby's behavior.

An important part of therapy with Mom involved helping her develop more self-confidence, less insecurity, and more assertiveness. Her lack of assertiveness was a weighty problem in her relationship with her husband, with other people in general, and caused her to be used at work. She needed to be more assertive with her son to control his aggression and his ADD behaviors. As therapy progressed she felt increasingly more self-confident and took considerable pride in repeatedly discussing how she had returned to a job as a manager, was in a position of responsibility, and how she had to learn to be more assertive with employees who were acting out. She talked of taking a management class and learning how to manage people on her job.

A major positive change in therapy came about when she and her husband were doing better in their marriage. They were able to "finally cut the coat strings" from her parents. She had relied upon them for some semblance of emotional support throughout the years when her husband was emotionally and physically unavailable.

Issues of self-confidence and insecurity were issues with both parents, especially the mother. She talked about a shy and unhappy childhood. She had grown up in a physically and emotionally abusive family, causing her considerable fear of aggressiveness by others. Her husband had demonstrated aggressiveness early in their marriage, and she was afraid of him. He had been verbally abusive to her. She talked about feeling helpless at times, being lazy, and being afraid of losing others' love. Some of Bobby's symptoms of saying he was "dumb and stupid" were described by mom as her own feelings unconsciously expressed in Bobby for many years. Since therapy began, she had become increasingly on more of an even playing field with her husband and was able to confront him about his lack of responsibilities and involvement with the children. The parents' sexual relationship and overall level of intimacy improved. As therapy progressed she pridefully talked about losing weight. Her ability to confront Bobby's negative behavior improved, which was crucial, as she had not done that before and at times had just sunk into a helplessly overwhelmed state. In the beginning of therapy mom and dad denied any type of marital problems. In therapy mom was able to see how marital problems were very instrumental in causing Bobby's behavior.

One of the intriguing aspects of this case was the fact that Bobby had been so out of control in sessions with his mother. The first time he showed up with his father, who was initially reluctant to participate in therapy, Bobby was almost non-ADD with little evidence of defiance. He was attentive and engaged in conversation. There was an obvious disparity between his behavior with his mother and father and their control of Bobby's behavior. This is an observation I have made of other ADD children on numerous occasions. Mom would initially yell and scream as her best attempt to try to get Bobby to comply, and then she would just give up. She would do everything for him so she would not have to argue and could avoid a confrontation with him. As a result of mom's passivity and ineffectiveness, dad often became overly strict and harsh. There was a noticeable lack of positive emotional communication between Bobby and his dad with his dad being distant physically and emotionally.

Dad was not only physically distant because he was a truck driver, but he did not communicate verbally with mom at all. He was working sixty to seventy hours a week, and one of mom's earlier assertive events with her husband was to require him to be more involved with her and the family or they might consider divorce. Eventually an important junction in therapy came about when mom and dad told Bobby he was adopted and that his adoptive dad loved him. Around that time dad took a more positive interest in Bobby. He took a new job that enabled him to come home in the evenings and help out cooking dinner, cleaning around the house, and getting involved in Bobby's day-to-day homework. His father's control of Bobby's behavior was quicker and more powerful than any effect I'd ever seen from his taking Ritalin.

Much of the therapy involved both parents being able to grow emotionally. Bobby's dad talked about having a history of being irresponsible, "drinking and having long hair," being prejudiced, and needing to "grow up" himself. The couple talked about how things were rapidly changing with dad's new involvement. He made a conscious and willing attempt to be more of a "father." This had "taken their relationship to a new level," according to mom. Mom felt freed up to pursue challenges, which enhanced her self-confidence at work in her new role as manager. The parent's marital relationship improved, and Bobby's behavior in school and grades got considerably better. Dad eventually took even more responsibility in his parenting role, becoming not only Bobby's Boy Scout leader but the pack leader. Dad was an Eagle in Scouts, and he was now able to renew his interest through a relationship with his son. Toward the end of therapy dad talked about the important virtues of being a Boy Scout, responsibility, honesty, and the Scout promise, which Bobby came in one day and proudly recited. Dad had also talked frequently about problems at work, getting along with others who exhibited rebellious and irresponsible behavior, which was symbolic of his own ability to work out Bobby's problems with rebellion and defiance at home and in school. Themes throughout their therapy involved work relationships and how those paralleled their improved marital relationship and parenting relationship with Bobby.

Toward the latter part of therapy, Bobby was mainstreamed out of full-time special education classes and his emotionally handicapped class, and he began to appear on the A honor roll. One of his later report cards revealed all A's and one B with positive teacher comments such as "displays a positive attitude," "demonstrates good work habits," and "a pleasure to have in class." General classroom behavior grades were A's, and he receives mostly A's in all classes to this day.

One of the dynamics frequently occurring in families with ADD-behavior problem children is the disparity between mom and dad, with one being too punishing and the other being too lenient in an effort to counterbalance each other. One parent displays continual passivity while the other shows over-responsibility for the child. As with Bobby's family and many others, there is a continual inconsistency with regards to rules and structure and making a child responsible. Later in therapy Bobby's parents were able to take a more honest and accurate approach to their familial problems. They were able to see things from their own locus of responsibility for Bobby rather than exhibiting such defensive and externalized blame toward the school and denial of marital and interpersonal problems in themselves.

Once I used an analogy about how a parent teaches a child to brush their teeth at night is the same problem as a child needing to learn to sit at their desk in school and do their math work properly. This was helpful as we described mom and dad's initial concerns about not being able to control Bobby in class, only when he was at home. This was resolved by teaching them that they would have plenty of opportunity at home to work on his teeth brushing and other aspects of the problem that would then eventually transfer to school. They made Bobby more responsible for doing better in school by getting daily behavior reports back from the teacher. With dad's increased interest in his school behavior, they made behaving well in school contingent on playing Nintendo or Sega. They were psychologically strong and resolved at that point to carry out consistently the consequences of Bobby's "choice" of behavioral responses in school. I often teach parents they will develop more behavioral control in their children by increasing their own effective control over the child. They can do this by setting up consequences for a child's choices so the child cannot lose and is thus motivated to act non-ADD. All parents are motivated by "good" and "bad" consequences for their behavior. Our job is to make children play by the same rules of the game of life that we do.

They went from being very angry, blaming, and ineffective parents to being responsible and involved. Much of the therapy with Bobby's family involved his mother and father coming to sessions. Occasionally one or the other parent would show up because the other had to work. Bobby was involved frequently, as was his younger sister. His younger sister also became more responsible, a good student in school, and without any behavior problems. The parents would often describe how they were using the same responses to Bobby as they did with her. They just had a chance to start off with Bobby's sister's "training" at an earlier age. As the parents became more educated about the causes of Bobby's behavior problems, they began to talk more about what they had learned with relatives and other family members and were able to give handouts to parents and to Bobby's school teachers.

I often give parents about twenty articles and papers about ADD and Ritalin controversies, including some good books as references. Often parents don't realize there's even a difference of opinion about ADD and its causes and treatments. Many physicians can be quite sensitive about a parent seeing me when they've told them something quite different from what I've told them. This is usually handled best by telling parents we all have opinions, and it's their responsibility to look at all available data and make up their own mind about how to proceed with their child. I won't tell parents to stop giving their child Ritalin. I simply tell them that if they're doing what needs to be done in therapy, then at some point their child will get better and they may find there is no longer any need for Ritalin. The decision to increase or decrease their child's use of Ritalin is between them and their prescribing doctor. This avoids the problem of non-physicians giving "medical" advice to parents, while at the same time one can tell a parent to read whatever they wish that is "psychologically" relevant. Sometimes children come from such out-of-control parent-child relationships that Ritalin is used by parents until they can develop much healthier and more effective control; but I've never recommended a parent seek medication in the last ten years of my practice. Parents are responsible for their day-to-day choices about their children. I'm responsible for the therapy, which when done correctly and when a parent is willing to cooperate, provides improved parental responsibility for day-to-day choices.

After three years of weekly family psychotherapy, Bobby's family became happier in many aspects. They took their first family vacation, which was a successful time for Bobby and his father, who found time to joke around and play and have a more mutually satisfying relationship. As for Bobby's parents, they came to enjoy having Bobby as their son.

12

Mark—A Parent's Introspective Changes

Mark was seven years old and failing first grade. His teacher sent several deficiency notes home, and at school conferences his mother was told that Mark could not pay attention in class, keep on task, or finish his work assignments. Mark was diagnosed with ADD by the school psychologist and was referred to a family doctor, who prescribed Ritalin. No other treatment was recommended to the parents by the school or by the doctor. Several months later the mother met with the same doctor to discuss some more recent concerns, and he suggested counseling, referring her to me. Mark and his mother were given psychological evaluations. After the evaluations were complete, his parents, along with Mark, met with me to discuss how to best help his family. They agreed to meet with me once a week to work on the problems the family was having. It was agreed Mark did not have to attend the therapy sessions. We discussed how a child's behavior can be altered by the parents' experience of receiving help. ADD behavior is most often learned or developed within the parent-child relationship; therefore, his parents were asked to consider if the way they related to their child could possibly be having an impact on his behavior.

Mark's mother thought issues in her life might be causing some problems, but she did not seem sure. After a few weeks of therapy she struggled with the decision to take Mark off Ritalin. This was a crucial decision for the mother. If she decided her son's problems were not due to biochemical imbalances but rather some deeper underlying issues going on within the family, she would have to take a closer look at her own life in order to help Mark. This posed a threat for the parents, but with supportive therapeutic help, issues were worked through and Mark's behavior improved. His mother chose to take him off Ritalin, and as the therapeutic process unfolded, the dynamics of the relationships within the family were found to have direct impact on Mark's failure in school.

The bad reports Mark's teacher sent home triggered his own mother's feelings of worthlessness and shame she had felt as a child. She had done very poorly in school and had suffered a great deal of humiliation and shame, so she unconsciously identified with Mark and did not want him to experience the same painful feelings she had felt. In her effort to spare him, she tried to help him with his work, finding her own fear of his failure and the resulting feelings caused her to become anxious and easily angered while trying to work with him. The stress created anxiety in Mark; as a result, he continued to perform poorly in school despite his mother's help. Consequently, this deepened mother's fear that her son would suffer as she had suffered and left her feeling helpless and depressed because she could not help her son. It became clear the mother had made the decision to medicate her son in an effort to save them both from having to face deeply painful feelings that needed to be explored.

Mark's mother took a more active role in therapy, although the father also attended. According to his mother, the situation was the same in the home. Mother felt responsible for Mark's problems and for most of the family issues, and she would often become stressed and anxious carrying the burden with little help from her husband. The underlying cause was an unconscious desire to maintain control, as a way for her to feel safe in her own home. After exploring some of her childhood fears arising in her troubled family, she discovered that in order for her to minimize the danger she felt, she would try to take total control of her environment. Once in control of all possible situations that could go wrong in the family, she would feel safe. Fear makes us feel powerless and vulnerable, and we try to figure out ways to protect ourselves. These unconscious strategies were carried into the present family dynamics. Through the therapeutic process, she became aware of what she was doing and learned that the existence of pain and sorrow in her childhood family was embedded deep within her person. Her efforts to control the external environment and the people around her was never an effective way to cope with fear. As she worked through her fear and began to understand it better, she was able to let go of some control in her family, which allowed her husband to take a more active role in the home and in his relationship with Mark. In addition she realized she was often jealous of any time her husband spent with Mark. She had grown up in a home where there never seemed to be enough attention for anyone, and she had carried this belief into her present family.

Mark's mother grew to understand that there were, indeed, creative ways to help each person in the family receive the attention needed. She and her husband made an extra effort to spend time alone together by going out on dates, and they learned it was all right to tell their children that they needed time alone to talk. It has been found that if the relationship between the parents is thriving and healthy, the children typically will be happier. In addition, the family made special days where each parent would spend the day with each child, giving the children the individual attention they needed. They also found ways to spend time together doing fun activities. This gave Mark the time and attention that he needed from his mother as well as his father, to thrive and develop a healthy self-concept.

As Mark's mother worked to develop a closer relationship with her family, she struggled with issues of intimacy and trust. Sexually abused in her childhood, she unconsciously avoided contact with her son. It triggered uncomfortable feelings within her she was trying to keep buried. She allowed these feelings to come up in the therapy process and was able to explore them. She began to work through them and develop a more affectionate relationship with her son, which helped improve his sense of safety and security; her relationship with her husband also improved greatly. She found that she was more relaxed with Mark. She became aware of often displacing her anger onto her son for issues she felt toward her husband. In the past she had learned it was easier to be angry at Mark. He would not reject her; she felt her husband might. Her experiences in her childhood home had taught her that if she said or did the wrong thing to someone she depended on, she might be abandoned. She developed a new sense of strength within herself, and her fear of abandonment diminished, and she was able to communicate openly and honestly with her husband, diminishing her displaced anger at her son.

Mark was not the only one to benefit from the therapeutic process; the whole family became happier. As his mother explored her relationship within the family and learned of the unconscious drives carried from her childhood home into her present relationships, she was able to create healthier relationships within her family.

When the parents started therapy, Mark was taking Ritalin and had completed first grade by attending summer school. When he entered second grade and was no longer taking Ritalin, but he was in learning disabled classes. Within the first year a notable improvement was seen in his school work. Towards the end of second grade, the parents scheduled a conference with the school to discuss taking Mark out of the learning disabled classes and putting him back in the mainstream classroom. The teachers recommended that he stay in the learning disabled classes and told the parents he would probably always have difficulty learning. The parents refused to believe this. They had come to understand that the adjustments made within the family were significant enough to help Mark develop the attributes he needed to succeed in school. Against the school's wishes, they took him out of the learning disabled class. They discovered he had not been working at mainstream second grade level because he had been in learning disabled classes for the entire second grade year. They chose to have him repeat second grade, this time in the mainstream class. Mark was on the honor roll throughout that year and continued to be an honor roll student years after therapy was completed. Mark became the quarterback of his football team, and active in other school sports. Teachers never sent home behavior problem notes, and all his teachers stated he was a wonderfully behaved student. Many years after his parents' therapy, Mark continues to be non-ADD-behaviored, and what his teachers, parents, and I would consider to be a very psychologically healthy, normal child.

13

Susie—ADD and Bipolar Disorder

Susie, a ten-year-old fifth-grade girl whose biological parents were divorced and geographically separated, was living with her natural mother and her stepfather out of state. There was a lot of conflict between Susie and her stepfather, and she was very negative about him. There was evidence of some physical and emotional abuse, such as the children being locked in a closet for various periods of time. Frequently she would become very aggressive with angry outbursts, physically hitting her parents. When her parents didn't follow through on promises (apparently her mother was often guilty of this), she would become particularly upset and angry. Her mother and stepfather argued too much, and she would be very mad when they would try to boss her around too much. She perceived that her parents did not understand her and had occasional outbursts of wanting to kill her sister. There was too much hitting and yelling in the home, and she sometimes wanted to run away. Her problems became so severe that she came to live with her natural father and his girlfriend.

Susie had been in psychiatric treatment for a few years, and had seen three different psychiatrists for a lot of behavioral and emotional problems. She had been diagnosed with bipolar disorder and attention-deficit/hyperactivity disorder, and had been taking Lithium and Ritalin daily for at least a year and a half. She had also seen a mental health counselor for weekly therapy for a few months. Susie spent six weeks in a psychiatric hospital after threatening to stab her sister with scissors.

The father's girlfriend brought Susie to see me. She proved to be easily irritated, often had pressured and rapid speech, and was sometimes sad and tearful. Easily bored, she was restless and fidgety at times, had trouble staying seated in church, and was easily distracted. She had difficulty following through on instructions, very often refused to do chores at home, talked excessively, would interrupt others, seemed self-centered and preoccupied with getting her way, and was bossy in her play with other children. Other problems were stealing, lying, jealousy, temper, aggressiveness, and frequent disagreements with her parents. She was often viewed as "having a mind of her own" and tending to be quite defiant and oppositional. She exhibited poor grades in school, although there was no diagnosed learning disability. When I saw her, she obtained average I.Q. scores and academic achievement scores at or above grade-level expectation. Nevertheless, her grades were D's and F's.

Psychological testing of Susie revealed a lot of negative perceptions of others. She was prone toward viewing others as being critical, feeling teased a lot, and having trouble keeping friends. She perceived others as either all good or all bad. She demonstrated some awareness of herself as being mean and having a temper. She displayed a significant tendency toward somatization through developing stomach pains, eye trouble, and headaches. Corroborative information from one psychiatrist, after she came to live with her father, described her as getting angry and wanting to hurt herself, but never attempting suicide. She had thoughts of strangling herself because she "couldn't take the pain anymore." Name calling, hair pulling, and allegations of punching and kicking by the stepfather were noted. She had bad dreams precipitated by watching horror movies in her mother's home. Her maternal grandmother was described as being abusive, threatening to hang her sister from the ceiling fan and locking her in the closet. Marks from being slapped in the face, repeated incidents of notifying the counselor at school, and once even calling Social Services on her stepfather were noted. One psychiatrist diagnosed her with attention deficit disorder, dysthymia, and post-traumatic stress disorder (PTSD). Functional enuresis was evident. The psychiatrist did not view her as having a bipolar disorder and attempted to take her off the lithium she had been on for about a year and a half to two years. A lot of behavioral and emotional problems were evident, and it was obvious Susie was reacting to many years of family turmoil.

Susie quickly showed a fond attachment to her father's girlfriend and viewed her as a mother-like figure, although she worried a lot about her mother and not being able to see her after going to live with her father. Susie would tell the girlfriend she loved her. The girlfriend was equally pleased as well as anxious to have "her own little girl to show off." She welcomed Susie into her home, complimenting her on her ability to be "a brave little girl who left her mother and family situation to get on a plane and come down by herself into a new living situation." She cared a lot about Susie and came with her for treatment. Dad's girlfriend was concerned with Susie being burdened by guilt, jealously, and resentment about various problems in her previous home. Susie's "new mother" had a child diagnosed ADD when she was younger, and now wanted to look at psychological approaches rather than pharmacological intervention after realizing "there has to be a better way." Susie's father had been away a significant part of her childhood as he had a job requiring him to be gone a lot. At the time Susie came to live with them, her father was planning retirement from the job, and it was his intention to spend more time with her. Initially the therapy involved Susie and her new mother coming in to talk about Susie's problems.

At the first interview Susie's grades had been mostly C's with a few B's and two D's. She was on 900 milligrams of lithium per day. There were no consistent dosage levels of Ritalin administered as it varied, and sometimes Susie refused to take it altogether. Her behavior in the initial sessions was very self-centered and stubborn, being friendly and engaging when she wanted to be. She showed poor frustration tolerance and lack of perseverance. She was impulsive and very physically active. It was difficult for her to sit still. She tended to avoid talking about feelings and thoughts with her new mother beyond a superficial basis. Eventually she became more verbal and willing to open up about conflicts in her previous home. Susie had been given "the run of the house" in a rather chaotic and dysfunctional family environment while she lived with her mother. As her father and new mother spent more time with her, they noted the considerable inconsistency with discipline and rules in the mother's home. There were also discrepancies between her father and his girlfriend in how much control she would have in her new home. Her new parents began to see improvements in her ability to be calmer, slow down in her talking, be less restless, execute more patience, and be more cooperative in getting her chores and school work done. Crucial issues in family therapy eventually arose when dad became more involved. All three of them came in on a regular weekly basis once his job situation changed.

There were times when Susie would obviously try her parents' patience with her defiance, and eventually her father had to put his foot down and became even more discipline-oriented. He let her know they loved her very much and they were not going to reject her, but there was no way they were going to let her get away with her horseplay and irresponsibility. They were "sticking to their guns" and forced her to be attentive and focused when she was mad and didn't want to be attentive. Despite the frequency and intensity of the blow-ups occurring between them, her parents knew they were not going to give up on her. They stuck with a "tough-love" parenting approach. They talked about the need for Susie to feel safe, have consistency, and live in a predictably loving environment. They became increasingly aware of their ability to meet these needs in their roles as parents. Differences in how mom and dad responded to Susie were identified, and they worked on becoming more consistent and agreed on how to administer punishment. Dad tended to be a bit more lax in punishment because of guilt about his absence and lack of influence in her earlier life. Mom was able to help develop an awareness on dad's part about the need to work together better and never allow dad's guilt about not being there for his daughter override the need for appropriate discipline.

Susie's parents became increasingly aware of the natural mother's irresponsibility and the extent to which Susie had been taught deceit. They focused on making Susie more honest and accountable for her actions. Psychologically, the natural father and her new mother seemed emotionally more stable in their own relationship and their lifestyles. There was relatively little arguing, yelling, or temper exchanged between the two parents; and both of them had a stable work history. They developed more interest in their religious practices and spent more time going to church. They worked on a relationship problem—fear of commitment—that existed between the two of them; and they became engaged and eventually married during the time of therapy. The marriage helped solidify their commitment to each other and to Susie, becoming a new family for her. Some issues revolved around mom's work stress. She increasingly recognized that work conflicts needed to be resolved and handled differently because they spilled over into her relationship with Susie. The parents found some hobbies and interesting activities for Susie, such as modeling, which allowed her to be on stage in a healthier manner.

Therapeutically they were expected to free associate and to communicate with each other. I said relatively little throughout the therapy process. Dad took this as an attempt to continually press Susie to talk about things and not allow her to say "I don't know" and remain quiet. A test arose around Christmas time after a year into treatment, they wondered if Susie would want to leave them and go back to live with her mother. Susie had old, unresolved emotional issues that surfaced then, causing her to feel the need to take care of her mother and siblings, to protect them. Dad was faced with an issue of people giving and getting enough attention in the family, and he was caught in the middle, having to placate both his wife and his daughter. Increasing conflict between mom and Susie came to the surface, and dad had to eventually side with his wife and provide a united front. Susie was challenging her as not being her mother, using that against her and trying to sabotage her authority. The parents had to resolve not to allow her to continue this behavior. Susie's role in the family and how much attention she was to be given versus dad's attention to his wife had to be worked out, so that Susie "knew her place in the family."

Dad was a quiet and introverted individual, and his wife tended to be somewhat quiet. Both had to learn to be more verbally expressive. Initially, as dad's girlfriend, his wife had to feel "authorized" to be given the role of disciplinarian, even though Susie rebelled against it. Later in therapy mom and dad were able to better define their roles, be more committed to each other, to get married, and take a more normal parental approach toward Susie. The realization that Susie was to be living with them until she was eighteen helped to further develop stability and predictability in the family. As mom and dad learned to be more consistent with rules, discipline, and expectations of Susie, her initial tendency to challenge their authority subsided, and she became more compliant and responsible. Dad was able to redevelop a more loving and positive relationship with Susie, and to be able to know when it was time to play and time to be a disciplinarian. Susie's stepmother felt more confident and supported by Susie's father and hung in there knowing they would eventually be able to turn Susie around.

At the age of 12, because of her improved behavior and a desire to be with her mother, Susie went for a visit with her natural mother, who had divorced the stepfather. She did not return for almost two years. During the two years her grades slipped. She was put into a special program for truant children after missing forty-six days in one school year. She became involved in gang activity, including smoking, drugs, sex, and stealing. When disciplinary problems became too much for her natural mother to handle, she was returned to live with her father and his wife. Upon arrival she was informed of family expectations of her. Her boundaries and expectations were spelled out. Within a short period of time her grades went back up. She stopped smoking and doing drugs and all other inappropriate behavior. He parents thought the "bottom line" was to reintroduce, in their words, "love, consistent standards, expectations, and discipline."

Susie came from a family situation that created her ADD behavior. She was geographically and psychologically moved into another family structure that was more stable, predictable, discipline oriented, and loving. As a result of change and working on specific aspects of reshaping her ADD behavior, she eventually became no longer ADD, bipolar, or oppositional-defiant disordered; and treatment goals were met. Eventually Susie's grades in school remained at the A-B honor roll level, and she no longer received behavior problem reports from her teacher. At home she was responsible and got her chores done, and she and her parents actually looked forward to more positive and healthy family time together. Susie was no longer as self-centered, hyperactive, impulsive, and manipulative. A follow-up consultation with Susie's father five years later revealed that Susie's changes remained permanent. She was described as "just a super kid." She continued to be on the A-B honor roll, was taking honors classes, and was a very likable and much more psychologically healthy child. When asked what they thought was most important in their treatment experiences, the parents stated it was definitely the consistency and structure that they were able to develop with more effective discipline. They stated with pride that "now when she feels she might get into trouble, she'll even come and ask us and say, 'I need more structure.' "

14

John—Parent Anger and Marital Problems

"This little man, he has violent outbursts. He punches, kicks, abuses his private caretakers, teacher, and baby-sitter. When he gets angry he'll throw chairs or whatever he can get his fingers on. It comes with no warning. They don't see it coming, either. He's lessened and matured a little bit over time so it's not to the degree it used to be. They're ready to move him again in school. He was recently moved to be with another preschool teacher because of his behavior. We've tried everything. We've tried all the behavioral techniques—charts, points, punishment, time out, you name it. Often things will happen at nap time. It's going on, like, daily. Now it's not every day, though. There have been longer spurts when it's been better. The teachers have worried about their safety. We've had a couple of other people, and they're already labeling him and wanting us to try medication. I said, "Hello!" and asked if there was some kind of a trainer or child development specialist that observed his classroom. We had a meeting. She recommended we go to a smaller environment.

He's had this behavior for a long time. I don't know what to do. My arms are up in the air. He'll even make the teacher cry. She'd get kicked, and he punched her. It seemed to be only her, though. He doesn't act aggressively with other kids. It's been going on with her for at least five or six months. He went to one psychiatrist for one session. She'd seen both of my kids at that point. She just wanted to put him on medication."

These were the words of John's mom. He was only four years old when she brought him to see me.

Mom described the differences between herself and her husband. She said dad would never spank John, merely send him to his room and tell him to "Knock it off!" or "Stop it!" Mom stated she was the same way, except if John took it to the limit she would spank him, though she hardly ever did spank him. Mom and dad's marriage was described as "doing real good. We have open communication. We always have. We'll talk about anything. We hardly ever fight, except about money. Bob is really laid back. I'm more aggressive. I'll raise my voice. I do spank. I do yell sometimes."

We talked about John's brother, who was a few years older and doing reasonably well, but had some of the same behavior problems. She described the brother as "a bit more quiet." The older brother also had trouble going to day care. He wouldn't stay in the class. Once in a while he would take off and run away, and the day care workers would have to chase him. Even so, the brother was doing pretty well academically in school.

Mom thought John's problems began one year prior. She said he used to be a happy and smiling child. She thought the problem began when he was moved to another class in school. She then spoke of the people in the day care center complaining about his being impulsive, not listening, and being too active. The problems at school seemed to escalate when Bob, her husband, would go away on a job assignment.

Often I have found that the initial consultation with one or both parents reveals much more psychological information about themselves and their child than can be obtained by simply giving them questionnaires or forms to fill out. But sometimes putting things down on paper or a subjective checklist or questionnaire to complete is different than what is verbally expressed in an interview.

I gave mom some behavior rating scales to be completed by herself, her husband, and the teacher. I gave them the Personality Inventory for Children to complete. For mom and dad, I gave them personal problem checklists to provide me with more information about their general psychological state. I requested her to fill out more forms because she described very few problems in her marriage. In addition, I wanted more specific information about problems in her son.

On our second appointment I reviewed the information John's mom brought back to me. The teacher described John as being impatient, unwilling to wait in line, had trouble waiting his turn, talked inappropriately, changed moods quickly and unexpectedly, called out and made noises in class, frustrated easily, acted without thinking, disrupted other children's activities, got into fights with others, was aggressive or violent, ran about or climbed on things excessively, and acted in a loud and noisy manner. A baby-sitter who also filled out the behavior rating scales responded similarly, stating he was inattentive and easily distracted, impulsive, and hyperactive. Mom and dad did not see him as being hyperactive or easily distracted and inattentive, but they did see him as impulsive. They agreed he would act before thinking, had difficulty waiting his turn in games or group situations, was impatient, talked out inappropriately, changed moods quickly, did not seem to listen, acted in a loud and noisy manner, and was aggressive or violent. Information on another behavior-problems checklist revealed even more. He often cried and was clingy to his parents. He didn't want to be alone and was afraid to do new things on his own. He was often afraid of new situations and strangers. He was irritable and easily upset. He was sassy to adults. He tended to lie a lot. He was prone to frequent temper tantrums. He needed the lights on to sleep in his bedroom at night and had been difficult to toilet train. I also learned his parents often disagreed about how to raise the child.

The information obtained thus far revealed many psychological problems and allowed us to expand upon the need to discuss issues with mom and dad and how they related to their son. John was easily diagnosed with ADD, based on a variety of behavioral problems as well as his significant difficulty with expression of anger. His mother and father were at the point that they had to do something because of his inability to remain in school and day care. He had apparently become so disruptive that the day care facility called in a behavioral specialist to observe and document his behavior. Mom was quite perturbed and had threatened to take legal action because of how the school handled the situation. After observing him for only four hours, the behavioral specialist told her John should be put on medications and removed from school.

John came to see me by himself for a session, and we did some projective personality tests. He tended to become aggravated when asked to elaborate on responses. He was unmistakably restless if he didn't know an answer. He was typically compliant but was often antsy and impatient on his effort to approach various tasks. When a task became too difficult, he grew uneasy and would lose all interest in trying, but with encouragement he would work quite well. He become irritated if he had to repeat his answers. He would make impulsive statements. For instance, if he didn't want to do a task he would state, "Then I'll just jump in the water, and the sharks will get me." On other projective tasks it was obvious that he tended to perceive people as being mean to him, and made impulsive statements that he hated his mother, at other times that he loved her. He stated he wished he could stop being mean to his mother and father. He thought he was different from others because he was bad. He said girls thought he was a monster and made other aggressive, impulsive statements. On a sentence-completion item, "It hurts when. . . ," he answered, "when I stick a knife in my pants. I'm just making it up." He would often give an answer and then say he was just making it up. He viewed his teacher as "dumb, dumb, dumb." He spoke of thoughts about monsters. He clearly demonstrated a lot of aggressiveness, insecurity, impulsive responding, and tension.

Information from the personal problems questionnaires, completed separately by mom and dad, revealed that dad complained of having marital problems. He was worried whether his marriage would succeed and was also worried about another family member. There were no other problems listed on this 288-problem questionnaire, which covers all aspects of one's life from physical and medical health to hobbies and interests, relationships with others, feelings about one's self, family problems, love and sexuality, philosophy of life and religion, and other aspects of day-to-day living. On mom's checklist, she described problems with dealing with her own anger, feeling drained, unhappy too much of the time, being nervous and high strung, feeling like a failure, worrying about her marriage breaking apart, being stubborn and obstinate, and not having enough personal freedom. She further expressed that she was dissatisfied about finances and with her current job, was feeling different from others and confused about what she really wanted, was lacking ambition, sleeping poorly, and having a lot of religious conflicts about the existence of God.

Mom summarized the way she and her husband had tried to handle John's problems, thus far without any success, as "therapy, punishment, time out, privileges taken away, loss of field trips, suspension, and constant reminders." I discussed with her the need to include dad in our work. Dad was in the military and often gone on temporary duty assignments, especially in the previous years. Now he was expecting to be home more, and it was prime time to include him in our therapeutic work. There was some initial reluctance on his part, but I was able to meet with both of them. They seemed relatively willing to talk about John's behavior, but it took a few sessions to focus more closely on the very significant marital problems and mom's depression and dissatisfaction with their marriage. She was characteristically anxious and animated during sessions, somewhat ADD in her own behavior, while dad was quite passive and low-key but talked. Both parents were willing to talk and free associate. Eventually dad did not come into the therapy sessions as frequently as mom. It was her impression he was just not interested, not only working on the problems with their son but in their marriage. John's behavior improved when mom and dad were able to talk about working together in their parenting. We were able to focus later on mom's depression and how to reduce her overall level of anxiety, anger, and dissatisfaction in her life. As we were able to help her calm down and feel happier, more self-confident, and controlled, so too was John's behavior correspondingly less aggressive and ADD.

At one point in the therapy dad gave the impression he thought mom needed individual therapy assistance. While this bothered mom, she was willing to continue and "take the matter into her own hands." In my approach with mom and dad, I was careful to continue to leave the door open for dad's involvement. I also supported mom's role in the relationship as the one who was most hurting and, therefore, the one who was able to provide positive change and motivation to get to the bottom of her son's difficulties. She struck me as a very psychologically-minded and assertive woman who was too depressed and unhappy in her marriage to be able to separate her feelings in that relationship from those toward her child. She had been overwhelmed at times in the beginning of therapy that she felt her life was too fragmented. She talked about all the responsibilities placed upon her as a mother and having to contend with problems with her husband (such as not being able to trust him and his excessive spending of money). We were able to delve into the psychopathology in her childhood experiences to look at earlier traumas that effectively molded and shaped her to be unhappy and inhibited the development of her self-confidence. We talked about her inability to become calm and less ADD in behavior. Early in therapy, as mom felt more understood and listened to, and as she and her husband worked together on their team approach to parenting, John's ADD behavior, and aggressiveness in particular, subsided quickly.

The therapeutic task became, to improve the parents' marriage and develop a calmer, more stress-free existence in mom. However, we were unable to see therapy through to its completion to resolve all of mom and dad's marital problems because of a job change requiring the family to move out of state. The parents' marital relationship was still somewhat up in the air although they had long since been able to teach John to act non-ADD. He eventually became very pleasant, sociable, sensitive to others, and exhibited no further aggressive outbursts. The overall length of therapy was approximately two years at the time they moved; and I would say that about six months to a year into the process John's behavior was significantly altered, and he was reshaped into acting much more non-ADD. A follow-up phone consultation with his parents a couple years later revealed their perception that "John was doing just great." He was getting A's and B's in regular classes in school. They had no more problems with aggressiveness. He was described as happy, well-liked, and one of the leaders of his class. There were no other problems expressed by teachers or other adults about John's behavior. His parents stated, "John has become a 'normal' charming young man. . . . He is active in sports, doing very well in school, has many friends, is very outgoing and polite, listens and completes tasks as instructed, and he exhibits no ADD behaviors."

John was fortunate to be at a young enough age with psychologically-minded and caring parents who knew there was something wrong about their child's behavior and were unwilling to drug him. They had the motivation to pursue weekly family and individual psychotherapy to separate out their son's needs from their own difficulties. Mom found a more satisfying career when they moved out of state, and that helped her feel better about herself. In addition she gained insights through more thoroughly examining her childhood problems in her family, which related to how she responded to John when she became upset. Her own anger and depression were resolved significantly through therapy, and in turn so were her son's. The parents also stated,

> You know I always hated the ADD label. . . . I think young children are trying to figure out where they stand in this world, and are just unlearned in managing their behaviors. When children continue to evolve and learn through teaching, experience, growth, differentiating right from wrong, coupled with strong parental involvement and caring, the child will eventually sort out who he or she is and develop into the adult they will become.
>
> Unfortunately, not every child is born and/or raised in an environment that instructs them how to act by society's standard; therefore, they are labeled throughout their child- and adulthood. Most parents, teachers, and psychiatrists do not try to learn *why* the child acts ADD, they just want it to "go away" by medication, so they don't have to deal with it. I think the ADD label should be PPPDD. . . . Psychologist/Psychiatrist/Parent Deficit Disorder. They just want to drug, instead of understanding the child and teaching him or her how to manage or change such behaviors.
>
> I want to thank you for helping us sort out our own behaviors, so we could effectively help our children's. Keep up the nonmedication and labeling of children through writing and counseling parents, by providing the guidance to parents on helping themselves, so they in turn can help and instruct their children to manage their behaviors.

15

Willie—Divorced Parents Working Together

Willie was a six-year-old child referred by his family's doctor for problems at home and school. He was diagnosed as attention deficit disordered and demonstrated stress-related physical problems with headaches and stomach aches. He was having difficulty with his parents' divorce and conflict between his biological mother and father over parenting issues. His parents split up when he was ten months old, and his mother remarried three years later. She was medically retired with a vestibular disorder that caused trouble with unsteady gait and necessitated walking with a cane.

On our first consultation, his mother brought him in stating he had an attitude problem. He became aggressive with children in school, not only hitting them but taking things from them. He chose to play with younger children and had been described as emotionally immature all his life. He teased his two-and-a-half-year-old brother. He would bully other kids, becoming bossy and aggressive. He was a chatterbox, constantly talking, and would not listen. It was difficult getting him to focus and be attentive. He would cry easily and was too sensitive. There was concern that he would enter second grade and be described as a crybaby.

In the first grade he had to be isolated from other children. His mother had several conferences with his teacher and the school guidance counselor. He was bright but did not want to finish his work. His teacher observed that if he was interested in something he could attend to it, but that rarely happened. The teacher thought he was not doing it on purpose—he would become sincere and remorseful—but thought it might be another kind of problem, maybe ADD. His mother had been thinking of ADD as a problem for about a year and was concerned that Willie wasn't as happy or well adjusted as he might be. Report cards commented repeatedly about excessive talking, lack of effort, and the need for more self-control. He tended to act immature and infantile at times. At other times he could be mature and smart.

We reviewed Willie's behavior and examined his report cards. He was in the first grade and received an N (need to improve) in general classroom behavior with problems of excessive talking and needing to improve self-control, complete class work, and pay more attention during class. He also received N's in P.E. and handwriting with some U's (unsatisfactory) in P.E. All other grades were S's (satisfactory).

ADD behavior rating scales were completed by his mother, biological father, stepfather, and teacher. There was consistent agreement by all raters that he was impulsive, inattentive, distractible, kept repeating the same mistakes, and that he could follow instructions but it took "a hundred and ten percent of his concentration and [he] often forgets what he's doing wrong." He did not seem to listen, was easily distracted, had difficulty planning and organizing things, needed a lot of supervision, would call out in class and interrupt, and changed moods quickly and unexpectedly. They all agreed these problems had been ongoing for about a year. It was noted he often complained of various physical aches and pains, seemed sad and unhappy at times, would easily cry frequently, and was often irritable and easily upset. Personality and projective tests were administered and confirmed problems with irritability, emotional immaturity, bossiness, oversensitivity, temper tantrums, conflicts in relationships with others, perceiving that others didn't like him, awareness of being mean and aggressive with other kids, and being sad and having difficulty in his family situation. His problems were described as being in existence since at least preschool. There was an indication his complaints of headaches and stomach aches occurred when he didn't want to do something.

Biological mom and dad were both seen initially. They complained of disagreement about finances and other aspects of parenting. Step-dad had also stated some marital tension and stress as well as work stress. There was complaint that the biological father did not spend enough time with Willie. There was further concern that the younger brother received more attention because he was the parents' biological son. From the beginning, the mom admitted the step-dad was rather stern and she was a pushover. She stated, "I know that is not good. We need to be more consistent with Willie, and we need to talk more before we instill some punishment."

Willie's medical history was reviewed, and it was essentially noncontributory. No significant pre- or perinatal birth complications or conditions were evident. Bilateral PE tubes for chronic ear infections had been placed early on, and he had some trouble with hearing and a ruptured eardrum.

Further review of the family history revealed step-grandparents being involved with Willie, and their treating Willie and his younger brother unfairly. There would be a lavishing of attention on the younger brother. There was significant jealously on Willie's part toward the brother.

At the time Willie was referred, his mother had considered a prescription for Ritalin, but his father was quite against it. I was able to have both sets of parents (father had also remarried) meet for a few visits to talk about the importance of developing a consistent game plan upon which all adults would agree about how to respond to certain important aspects of Willie's day-to-day behavior. All four seemed genuinely interested and willing to sit in the same room and talk about Willie, which made therapy work more effectively.

Different perceptions on biological mother and father's part about time spent with Willie, who allowed whom to spend time with him, and stepfather's involvement or lack of involvement with Willie were discussed repeatedly. As therapy progressed, there seemed to be a better working through of the time Willie was able to spend with his mother and father. Mom, on one hand, viewed the father as being allowed to have Willie whenever he wanted; dad viewed his time with Willie as significantly restricted. There were also concerns about what Willie was supposed to eat and who was responsible for holding him accountable for his homework.

In separate consultation with his mother and stepfather, we were able to take a look more closely at their marital problems. There were conflicts they did not want to get into with the biological father. We spent a lot of time talking about setting limits and boundaries with Willie, and appropriate punishments and responses when he acted out. In a very healthy manner, mom was able to realize she had been too lenient with Willie. Dad, at times, would back away from punishing because of concern Willie's mother would not agree with his responses. Issues of intimacy in their marriage were examined, mom's depression, dad's having to work a lot, and unresolved feelings from all parties about the divorce.

The divorce had been very tumultuous with a lot of legal investigation and court testimony leaving Willie's father feeling very resentful that primary custody was awarded to mom. When I met him, he eventually admitted he had become so angry and resentful that he had cut off contact with Willie. He realized he could not do that for Willie's sake, and became more involved in Willie's life during the time of coming to see me for therapy. I met with dad in collateral visits to talk more about his ability to become a father with Willie, and discussed strategies to respond to Willie's mom in a way to produce less conflict about parenting. Much of the initial therapeutic contact with dad was working through his resentment toward mom, the divorce, and the custody battle.

We decided to meet with all four parents to discuss the issue of Ritalin and medication. We were able to come to a consensus that we would involve all of them in the therapy process first before resorting to medicating Willie. They were all able to agree Willie needed more control and more structure in school work and his behavior. They all agreed he was not brain-impaired; and in fact, there were many things he was able to do, such as Nintendo or watch movies on TV, with considerable good attention and concentration.

About four months into the weekly family psychotherapy, it became more apparent that the natural father's anger and other issues regarding Willie would be better resolved through separate sessions. The marital issues and problems between mom and stepdad would be better worked through in sessions with them. We split them up and worked separately. At this point both sets of parents were feeling increasingly able to agree on school work and behavioral consequences, but other longer-term and more deeply troubling issues needed to be resolved to maintain permanent consistency in solving Willie's ADD behavior problems. Up to this point, all parents had been very willing to set aside animosity and concern about the other parties in order to come to my office and sit in the same room and discuss things. Unfortunately this is not a typical situation where there are differences between parents' views of the child's behavior and how to resolve problems.

Despite mom's initial misunderstanding about the nature and causes of ADD, she was in the mental health field herself and realized she had been given misinformation by her own psychiatrist. She was quite psychologically-minded and willing to consider problems from a psychological and parenting perspective. Eventually she was able to see that the obvious problems of inconsistency and lack of discipline were crucial. Dad also had been able to appreciate his need for more involvement in Willie's life. He took it upon himself to see that they talked about his schooling and homework, and made talking about school a mutually pleasant experience. This relieved the burden on mom to focus on other issues in her life. Step-dad had been very amiable throughout, even when discussing conflicts between his wife and her ex-husband. He had always been psychologically-minded about the importance of discipline and control and those things he intuitively felt from the beginning were validated through the therapy experience. He was able to take a more positively involved role in mediating conflicts. I was able to work through mom and step-dad's marital conflicts separately from dad's concerns about what he perceived as inadequacies on Willie's mother's part.

Willie continued to gain from our efforts. Early on during the sessions, Willie was noticeably improved in his behavioral response to all parents and teachers. About eight or nine months into therapy, there ceased to be any further problems at home or in school. Because of the willingness of all adults to set aside conflicts and work together, the therapy process moved considerably faster. They all obviously cared enough about Willie to examine their own feelings and form a necessary parent-child response to reshape Willie's behavior from being ADD to being non-ADD. Dad had to be assisted in learning how to respond to Willie in a more effective manner and not get caught up into all of the problems he perceived Willie's mother was causing in the situation. Mom needed help with being more encouraged and self-confident about the change process as well as her own ability to become happier and more satisfied in her current marriage.

Follow-up contact with Willie's parents a few years later revealed he exhibited no other ADD behavior problems. He remained an A-B honor roll student and was very well behaved in class. There were no more bad teacher reports, and at home he was compliant and did his homework on his own. His mother described him as their "little angel." The parents described therapy to be a very positive experience for their family. "Willie is now a healthy, well-adjusted 11 year old," they said.

16

Heather—ADD Parents

Heather, a 13 year old, whose behavior and school performance had not significantly improved after many years of regularly taking Ritalin, was referred by her pediatrician. This is a very common problem. Ritalin rarely provides completely satisfactory long-term benefits to most parents of children with ADD behavior.

Parents often come to therapy or counseling stating they want help with "other issues" like self-esteem or "learning problems," thinking their child is brain-damaged; but they use these terms to justify getting further help. After being told a child is brain-impaired, the parents' expectation of resolution of the ADD behavior problem often takes a back seat to the need to seek treatment. Parents simply label the presenting problem differently. Often practitioners and researchers will describe concurrent or "comorbid" problems with children, such as depression, adjustment problems, the need to learn to open up and communicate more, or the need to resolve their anger about something or someone. Most of the time these problems also exist in the parents and are projected upon the child. It is not unusual for a child to come in with a parent who states that the child needs to get over anger or feelings about being abandoned by the other parent, when it's the parent who also needs to do this.

It is not uncommon at all for parents to want to drop their child off with a mental health practitioner to be "therapized" or "counseled." Many times a parent will state the child needs to open up and find someone to talk to, or get something out, or express themselves. I consistently reformulate the problem to parents by stating that the child and the parent need to do these things with each other. Then my recommendation for family therapy will follow, with the parents needing to realize that they have to be able to draw out from the child what they expect the mental health practitioner to draw out, which is a more pervasive problem than the specific symptoms. Often parents will not want to do this, and then don't come back for treatment.

A lot of psychological counseling or therapy with children conducted by others involves individual therapy with the child or play therapy techniques, and I find this many times to be discouraging. It's almost as if there is an acceptance that a parent cannot learn to communicate with their child more effectively. It's been a long time since I've worked only with the child. This is not to say that individual therapy or work with children is unjustified or ineffective. I think, for the most part, it is limited because it avoids access to the more significant problems or pathology in the parent. There are cases wherein working "through" the child means going with the parents' resistance, though eventually a parent can be pulled back into treatment. Sometimes children are able to show important emotional and behavioral gains in individual therapy, but this is not the optimum situation.

In Heather's situation, her parents had been under the assumption that she was brain-impaired, and for many years that justified her taking Ritalin. When the Ritalin no longer worked, their doctor simply tried to find a different medication. In her case, they attempted Cylert, also without any significant benefit. Her parents thought Heather needed to talk with someone, and she had other "problems" of self-esteem needing assistance. When I interviewed Heather with her mother and father, the pediatrician had referred her for the purpose of an evaluation, particularly because of a decrease in grades to D's and F's after having been on Ritalin for many years.

On interview mom and dad stated,

> We need to get her calmed down again somehow so we can get the grades up. They were A's and B's, and now they are B's and C's, and she got two F's. We don't know if it's puberty or what's causing the problem. She doesn't follow things through. She's been on Ritalin since she was five years old. They increased the dosage since she got older. Then they put her on Cylert last year. She uses the medication as a crutch. We need to get her calmed down to follow directions and complete tasks she's told to do. I know she can do better, and so does she. It's a motivational type of factor—changing classes all day

> and having six teachers. Maybe her other school was behind. I don't know. We need guidance on how to calm her down medication-wise. She'll say she's not doing her best effort, and she'll just say she doesn't know. We'd never had the problems on Ritalin, and she'd do things and not have to be told what to do. It slowed her down enough. Then they took her off the Ritalin and put her on Cylert. She did get D's when she was still on the Ritalin. So we changed to Cylert and then her grades went up. Now they're going down again.

I then asked them if they had any other problems in the home or family, including marital problems. The parents stated, "No, that's about it." Then mom stated she was hyperactive and put on medication when she was in kindergarten. They then mentioned Heather's brother was hyperactive and having similar problems. Both parents still denied any kind of marital problems or distress.

Heather was subsequently administered various psychological tests. Her mother, father, and teacher completed behavior rating scales indicating that Heather was quite impulsive, inattentive and distractible, and hyperactive. These agreed with the pediatrician's subjective assessment. Heather had other problems with lying, moodiness, fine and gross motor skill deficits (difficulty cutting with scissors, running or riding a tricycle, and drawing neatly). Heather would also disobey her parents. She seemed to be rejected by other children and acted immaturely. She lacked self-confidence. Her ADD behaviors of impulsiveness, hyperactivity, and distractibility were present and documented from at least kindergarten. Other problems noted were lying her way out of trouble, feeling people are picking on her, not taking the lead in things, not waiting for things or being patient enough, being unable to sit still, and not getting along with other children. Sometimes she would appear sad or unhappy, and at times she would be afraid of new situations or strangers.

I reviewed Heather's past medical and psychological history. There were problems that were psychologically evaluated at age three, and significant marital problems with threatened divorce were noted. There had been concern from the Department of Children and Families about inadequate parental supervision in the home with Social Services being involved.

At my office Heather received average I.Q. test scores, and her academic achievement test scores were at her grade level expectation, except in writing. One test I have often used in research and clinically, the Matching Familiar Figures Test (Kagan 1964, 1965) revealed Heather to be impulsive and nonreflective. Drawings on the Bender-Gestalt Test and Human Figure Drawings revealed impulsive behavior. I have often used Human Figure Drawings and Bender-Gestalt Test drawings with children in research and clinical experience to show motor skills were also impulsively impaired. Psychological tests can be used to indicate problems of impulsiveness or lack of reflectivity, but this is not necessary for making a diagnosis of attention deficit disorder. I rarely perform psychological tests on children now, as there is plenty of information obtained through simply looking and listening how they behave with their parents.

During testing Heather was noted to have poor eye contact, acted somewhat immaturely, and approached tasks in a trial and error manner and sometimes with poor effort. At times she would guess haphazardly. She would jump from one item to another. She had to be busy and do something all the time. She fidgeted. She seemed nervous. She was imaginative and would tell stories about herself while performing tasks. She would play with Legos and crash them into each other, making noises.

I administered projective personality tests to Heather, and considerable family conflict was evident. A lot of preoccupation with impulsive behavior, aggressive concerns, throwing fits, having a bad temper, insecurity, thoughts about running away, resentment about her biological father, insecurity, depression, and generally a lot of psychological or emotional conflict existed. She stated that when she gets mad she'll hit anybody that messes with her, and it wasn't unusual for her to be depressed, have nightmares, think about running away, feel lonely and estranged from others. She viewed boys as thinking she was ugly. She viewed parents as yelling at her, arguing between each other, being too aggressive, and that her school teacher didn't like her. A lot of conflict perceived in relationships with people was evident. Her testing revealed she had many other problems, not just paying attention, concentrating, or being hyperactive. Further questioning about her brother revealed he had a lot of similar problems.

In the hundreds of psychological testing evaluations I've performed on children with ADD behavior problems earlier in my career, it has always been the case that these types of psychological and emotional problems exist to one degree or another but were overlooked in light of the more obvious presenting symptoms. There is always much more going on than meets the eyes of parents and their report of psychological functioning within the family.

I recommended to Heather's parents that family psychotherapy would bring about a much better resolution to her problems than Ritalin or Cylert. Heather's parents decided to follow-up with me for a second consultation. At our second consultation, both parents were present and revealed that, while they didn't have "marital problems," they did have differences of opinion or disagreement, a lot of stress in the family; and both mother and father worked far too many hours, with mom working almost double time. Heather stated, "We never get to see our dad because he's on day shifts, and when he's off he sleeps all day." To this, dad stated he would like to have better communication with his children. He and Heather's mother talked more about wanting to be able to have Heather complete tasks and not have to tell her seven or eight times. They mentioned the children were always fighting with each other and needed to settle down. They talked about the children blaming each other, and we were finally able to move into discussion of the parents having a lot of trouble with stress, disagreements, and temper. Dad was angry and frustrated, and mom was quite depressed. Both were experiencing a lot of conflict in their jobs, which frequently took them away from the children and overall family relationships.

The next follow-up consultation with both parents involved discussion of marital problems, the need for mom and dad to agree on how to discipline Heather and make her do homework, to determine who was going to take responsibility for seeing that she learned to do it on her own, and to increase communication with her teachers to get more feedback about what she was and wasn't doing in class.

In Heather's situation, both parents were quite ADD in their behavior, with mom being frequently a very tense and anxious person and emotionally volatile at times. She would frequently make impulsive statements during sessions. Dad tended to be a bit more low key, but he too was impulsive in statements. Sitting with Heather's parents felt like a tension-filled hyperactive encounter where I had great difficulty spending a lot of time focusing on the content and flow of their conversations, not knowing what would come next. At one moment everything would be "all right," and then the next moment there would be a "problem." There would often seem to be a crisis at work or at home. Initially, we spent considerable time talking about an episode of potential sexual abuse perpetrated by someone outside of the family. There was concern about dad losing a job, but the family was always in constant motion, with no sequential logic or framework.

I remember in the beginning thinking, "If I could just get mom and dad to come in, talk and free associate, and discuss things in a calm manner, this would in and of itself provide a more calming, less ADD-related behavior pattern in Heather." Much of the therapy was geared toward creating an environment wherein mom and dad could come in and talk without me getting particularly anxious or fettered by the disjointed quality of issues presented, and to allow them to develop a more calming, soothing, centered, and focused discussion of what to do about Heather. As mom and dad were able to work through marital conflicts, develop more of a consistent game plan on how to respond to Heather, and to "just mellow out," Heather learned to do the same.

Heather's family was characteristic of some families where both parents were just as, if not more, ADD-behaviored than the child. Therapeutic efforts focused on teaching mom and dad to be less ADD in their behavior and day-to-day lifestyle. Keeping therapeutic appointments consistent because of things getting in the way and numerous cancellations had to be resolved. In fact, they stopped treatment for extended periods of time on more than one occasion and then returned, at which point we picked up where we left off. To some degree mom and dad knew what they had to do, but needed someone to help them sit down and focus themselves on how to do it. Just getting a simple framework of a plan set up wherein Heather was expected to do her homework when she came home, rather than allowing her to go off and do whatever she wanted, was very helpful.

Heather had seen another therapist, but play therapy was the primary treatment modality. As with many parents, Heather's parents wanted me to "talk to her" at first, to work with her. I explained to them that if there was any difficulty in talking to Heather, it was part of their problem, and they needed to learn how to teach her to talk to them. Most of the sessions involved mom and dad coming to see me. When Heather did come in, she seemed to be non-ADD in her behavior. Her parents were able to control, discipline, and elicit appropriate responses from her quite well. It seemed more of a matter of her parents being able to focus their own time and attention on getting things done with Heather in the home rather than leaving her to fend for herself.

Mom and dad came up with a plan requiring her to do three hours of homework a day, whether she said she had homework or not. If she came home and said she didn't have homework, she would have to make something up. About three months into the therapy, Heather's Cylert was discontinued because they saw no benefit. Within the same time frame Heather's grades continued to improve as her parents focused on the homework solution. As mom and dad talked in sessions about how to make Heather more responsible, we talked about the parents learning to be more responsible.

Later in the therapy we focused more on the parents' difficulties in their work situation, where the father had conflict at the job with a supervisor, and another time with mom's conflict on the job with a supervisor.

Approximately two years later Heather's parents came back to see me. Previously they had left feeling that Heather was "on track," and they would be able to work things through on their own. They stated, "Heather has taken a left turn in her school work. We're trying to get her back focusing on tasks." They said her self-esteem was going down, and she wasn't applying herself. We talked again about picking up where we left off. We then met and talked about focusing, how mom and dad needed to do it; in their daily lives they had been unaware of just how unfocused and disjointed their work situations and family life were, having slipped back into the old pattern. Mom had been working 70-80 hours a week at work at the time, and they were having a difficult time with Heather. They mentioned at times she still got hyperactive and said, "Now we know where Heather gets it." Issues of dad being able to talk with mom and not have her feel so hurt or criticized by him needed to be discussed, which allowed them to move into the issue of self-esteem that needed to be improved in mom and in Heather.

As mom and dad focused on their own psychological problems with each other, Heather's behavior improved, and less attention was focused on her and more attention on them.

One of the difficulties in therapy with ADD-behaviored children is that the child has become the main focus of attention or "the identified patient or problem." When other problems, such as marital conflict or a parent's psychological problems, are the focus, the child improves. This happens because the parents are able to realize their behavior with the child varies depending on their spousal behavior with each other. Parents need to focus on their own problems, and separate out their parental role and responsibilities with their child.

I had contact with Heather's father a few years later, after she graduated from high school. He stated she had done "marvelously" since therapy was resumed. She no longer took any kind of psychotropic medications. She graduated from high school on the A-B honor roll. She no longer had any behavior problems in class as identified by teacher phone calls or behavior problems listed on report cards, and teachers were pleased by how well behaved she was in class. They said she'd done "quite a turnaround," and had "grown up to be a mature young lady." She was enrolled in college. I asked her father what he felt was most helpful in their therapy experience. He stated that he and his wife had to learn patience to deal with many aspects of their relationships, be appropriately critical of her, and to not accept "that was the way she was." To learn how to treat her like an individual rather than a robot. He said they needed to learn to be more responsible themselves before they could teach her to be more responsible with her school work. It was helpful to get her involved in structured activities like band and ROTC, to give her something interesting to look forward to doing. They saw value in developing more responsibility with her, to make her take responsibility for her actions and to put more effort in performing things, while they did the same.

17

Lisa—Adjustment to Divorce

Lisa was a seven-year-old girl who was in first grade. She was referred by her pediatrician after school teachers insisted that her parents seek consultation. According to parents and teachers, Lisa was unable to sit still for more than five minutes. She talked constantly, and the teacher was having problems keeping her in her chair and with her doing her work. She just wouldn't sit still. She had a short attention span, would talk back, call people names, and became disobedient at times. She tended to jump up and down on furniture. She wouldn't complete her chores. She was very whiny. She had difficulty managing changes, and the parents described that everything was a fight for her. She was argumentative, and she often did not listen when spoken to directly. She was not organized. She tended to lose things that were necessary for tasks, and she was forgetful. She was always on the go. She had difficulty waiting her turn. She would often interrupt and intrude on others or butt into conversations and games. There was no evidence of psychotic mentation or delusional thinking. There were no repetitive activities like rocking or headbanging. She did suck her thumb. She didn't try to deliberately hurt herself. She had no unusual fears. She did not become withdrawn and deliberately avoid people. There was no bedwetting. She did not lie, and she did not set fires. She did not run away from home or leave classes. There were no sexual preoccupations or problems. She was kind to animals and smaller children. She was not a bully. Lisa's extensive neurological and pediatric evaluation by her pediatrician was normal. Records from the school teachers who were suggesting Ritalin to the parents revealed two different common ADD behavior rating scales administered consistently showed significant problems in a variety of areas of inattentiveness, hyperactivity, and impulsivity completed by both teachers and parents. Notes from consultation with the teacher by the pediatrician and myself indicated one teacher had known Lisa for two years and stated she was distractible and impulsive during that entire time. It was not for just a few months at a time, as mom had initially presented to the pediatrician. Lisa had moments of defiance with particular teachers, but it wasn't a consistent or regular problem. No apparent learning difficulty was evident on school psychology testing with regard to I.Q. and academic achievement, which were all scored in the average range of ability.

My first interview of Lisa and her mother and father at my office was after she'd graduated from first grade. As both parents described Lisa,

> She just doesn't want to listen. She yells and hollers and won't do what we ask her to do without an argument. She can't sit still. She's little Miss Know-it-all. We've taken away the TV, grounded her, and nothing works. She's whiney, too. She talks nonstop. Other than that, she's just fine. She's still in the terrible two's. She gets S's in her school work except behavior. She gets N's. The teacher says she does OK with the work, it's just keeping her still to do it. We had company over the weekend, and she doesn't even have common sense enough to think about what she was doing. In school she doesn't sit still, and she forgets things. She's ditzy. She's always in trouble with the teacher. The other day she was caught in class reading and handing out and getting phone numbers of the other kids instead of studying.

The parents had been married and had Lisa the first year of their marriage. They subsequently were divorced when she was six, but had decided to live with each other for the two years preceding coming to therapy. Dad had moved out of the house once or twice during that time. They felt they wanted to make another go at their relationship. Mom had problems with arthritis, fatigue, and being depressed off and on for about eight or nine years. The father wasn't depressed, but he and she were in some physical altercations. He mentioned having a short temper. Mom would often yell at dad. There was a lot of yelling and arguing going on in the home.

Lisa was restless and fidgety during the interview and during psychological testing. On testing Lisa completed projective personality tests, and there was obvious conflict in the home and marital disagreement. On a follow-up consultation with Lisa's parents, we described Lisa's problems to be psychologically caused and that they could be psychologically resolved. Both parents were glad to hear that they did not have to put their child on Ritalin; and even though therapy would take some time, they would be able to solve the problem. I recommended to both parents that they see me together, and I did not see Lisa again during the therapy. After a few months of therapy, the parents reported improvement. Mother and father were acting more as a team rather than often fighting or arguing about differences in how to respond to Lisa.

One of the obvious problems in Lisa's situation was parental disagreement about how to respond to her, not just with discipline, but about homework, chores, and many aspects of her day-to-day life. We talked a lot about not letting Lisa manipulate both parents and get into the middle and be the focus of their disagreement, and we talked about how the parents could learn to work together for Lisa's benefit and set aside their marital disagreements. Dad became tougher on rules because mom tended to be more of the disciplinarian. There was less hollering and arguing about Lisa and how to handle her.

Eventually both parents decided that they did not want to live together, and that they would split up again and dad would move out. The parents were not experiencing significant success in their marriage or desire to stay together, but Lisa was doing better in school as a result of both parents being able to work together toward changing her behavior. Both agreed that sometimes, because of the nature of the problems between both mother and father, there had to be one primary disciplinarian in the home, which would be mother. This was decided upon in part because the father was often gone working (from the mother's perspective, too much), and he seemed to show relatively less interest in being around Lisa in a fatherly role. As the father's emotional and physical distance from Lisa increased, Lisa improved in school and her ADD behaviors decreased.

Both parents would still come to therapy, although later on during the course of our one-year treatment, dad did not come in, as it was made known that they were going to separate on a more permanent basis. At that point the father developed an interest in another woman, and the mother decided to focus more on parenting and her work. Mother's depression improved and she became more active, less of a homebody, and talked a lot in therapy about how to become more self-confident and assertive in relationship with others, particularly men.

About six months into therapy, Lisa's teachers and parents completed behavior rating scales, and there were no significant problems of impulsivity, inattentiveness, or hyperactivity evident. They reported improved progress in getting Lisa to complete homework, and her grades improved considerably from what were previously all F's and N's. At about ten months into therapy mother stated there were no longer any ADD behaviors confirmed by father and by school teachers, and Lisa brought in a report card with all A's and not one negative teacher comment. Instead, teacher comments were statements such as "a pleasure to have in class."

In Lisa's particular situation, both parents previously decided they did not want to stay married; and with the father's increasing absence from the home, Lisa's grades improved in part because of parental cooperation and more clear cut and agreed upon ways of relating to Lisa in her day-to-day behavior and school work. Mother's improved happiness and relative lack of depression and fatigue were also of assistance in giving her more energy to respond to Lisa's problems. They described that the father's derogatory and pessimistic or critical comments and attitudes toward Lisa no longer existed in such a significant manner. The father did continue to have contact with Lisa, but more time was spent with pleasant father-daughter activities rather than emphasis on discipline and in improving her sense of responsibility. Some of the therapeutic sessions with mother and father were more involved in clarifying what dad's role in Lisa's life would be, to the satisfaction of both parents.

While Lisa's case was a more obvious example of ADD behaviors related to parental conflict and disagreement, it is highly unusual to find effectively functioning marriages in any ADD-behavior-problemed child I've ever seen. Lisa's ADD behavior problems had existed for many years; With considerable cooperation between a mother and father, even those who had been divorced, their ability to set aside their own problems and to focus together on how to respond more appropriately can eliminate ADD behavior problems in a relatively short amount of time.

I followed up with Lisa's mother two years later. She happily reported that Lisa continued to be on the A honor roll, was in regular classes, was very well behaved and happy, and there were absolutely no negative reports of behavior problems by her teacher. Specific problems of detention, suspension, and notes sent home by the teacher were entirely absent in their day-to-day life. Her parents maintained more effective and agreed upon roles with her.

18
Conclusion

Things do not change; we change.
—Henry David Thoreau
(1854)

If there is anything that we wish to change in our children, we should first examine it and see whether it is not something that could better be changed in ourselves.
—Thomas Szasz
(1972)

Parents have a choice to make among all their other choices in their busy daily lives. They have to choose which professionals to believe about the nature of their child's ADD misbehavior. Even if they choose not to seek professional help, they have to make a choice about their child's ADD behavior. Because if they don't someone else—society or their own child—may make it for them. It is inevitable that all parents will have to modify, change, or shape their child's behavior one way or another.

Does a parent believe things that some professionals tell them, that their child has an innate biologically-based genetic or brain abnormality for which there is no cure, that they have to accept it and deal with it the best they can? Does a parent believe that it is only society, cultural factors, inept schools, or teachers that need to change rather than they or their child? Do they take another approach and believe their child's ADD behavior can change, but they need to drug their child, hoping that the child will grow out of it some day, or until some other means of solving the child's disposition occurs?

Whatever choice a parent makes, I hope they would read what everybody has to say about their child. Keep an open mind, think in more depth about the nature of their child's misbehavior. A parent has a choice about how they want to raise their child and what kind of person they want their child to become.

I have found that many mental health practitioners and researchers seem to be operating under the belief that misbehavior, and ADD in particular, is more under the control of genetics and neurophysiological braining functioning rather than human intelligence, willful choice, and the ability to think and discover psychological cures. Critics of my views may call me naive about their "scientific facts" to psychologically justify their attempts at perpetuating their own beliefs about the nature of why children misbehave.

Parents are often led to believe they are disempowered, without a cure in sight. They often embark upon years of treating their child as if they are either "special" or "disabled," rather than being empowered and supported in their capacity to be more effective and loving parents than they already are. The more parents are not held responsible for the behavior of their children and misbehavior is explained away through what at first glance seems like authoritative and compelling arguments, the more the epidemic worsens.

Solving the ADD behavior problem is all about developing structured discipline, consistency, and attentiveness to others. Curing ADD is a value-laden endeavor that seeks to develop or strengthen psychological variables such as respect for authority, self-discipline and control, other-centeredness rather than self-centeredness in life, and development of personal responsibility. The capacity to pay attention, to act reflectively and calmly rather than hyperactively, has to be taught to *all* children. These psychological processes are psychologically developed and central to a successful lifestyle. ADD behavior is governed by attitudes, perception, feelings, and beliefs about what is right and wrong in life, not in beliefs about disabled human beings.

Many parents know these things, but can be psychologically ill-equipped and disempowered by mental health professionals and the social views of the nature of child development. Parents must challenge prevalent views of human nature to determine what drives us and motivates. How much emphasis to put on biological, psychological, and spiritual realms of influence and their place in the development of ADD behavior in our children is crucial.

Getting help for your ADD-behaving child is more about teaching and learning than making excuses and accommodations for the child. It is less about blaming parents than it is about holding them responsible and equipping them with the necessary educational tools. It is more about developing changed habits and life-long behavior patterns than about quick fixes and attractive short-term solutions.

Parents, develop your own ongoing beliefs. Educate yourself. Read John Rosemond's books on parenting, David Stein's book on parenting, and Peter Breggin's many books on how so many otherwise knowledgeable and caring professionals have misguided beliefs about the nature of ADD-behaving children. Seek out professionals in your own community who share the belief that all children can learn and grow, and all parents can learn to teach them to do so in the most psychologically healthy manner possible.

This book provides very compelling scientific facts and clinical observations about the nature of ADD-behavior change, which are consistent with research on normal child development and growth, what many psychotherapists and counselors already know and do, and resonate with what parents intuitively and faithfully believe in their religious practices geared toward developing more spirituality and meaning in their life. To those who are still convinced of the other views of human nature, be patient. Time will tell. We are currently in the midst of a historical swing in the nature of scientific and clinical thinking and practice. The 1990s were touted as the "decade of the brain." I am always intrigued to find out anything that neuroscience can tell us about genetics and how the brain functions. But try not to confuse or misinterpret interesting research findings, or what brain processes are *correlated* with psychological functioning versus what researchers try to tell you *cause* psychological functioning. The Human Genome Project is intriguing, and it's interesting that we can clone sheep; but it is unreasonable and undesirable to assume that we could also clone non-ADD behaving children. All children grow up naturally being curious, stimulus seeking, investigative, and ADD in their behavior. Parents and civilized society mold, shape, and ultimately can have more control over behavior. There is too much drugging of children, delinquency, and violence caused by disempowering parents and abdication of responsibility. Join me to do all we can to support parent-child relationships and healthier families. We can do better than some people think.

Bibliography

American Academy of Pediatrics (AAP). 2000. "Practice guideline: Diagnosis and evaluation of a child with attention-deficit/hyperactivity disorder." *Pediatrics* 105: 1158–70.

American Psychiatric Association (APA). 1989. *Treatment Of Psychiatric Disorders: A Task Force Of The American Psychiatric Association*. Washington D.C.

American Psychiatric Association (APA). 1994. *Diagnostic and Statistical Manual of Mental Disorders: Fourth Edition (DSM-IV)*. Washington, D.C.

American Psychiatric Association (APA). 2000. *Diagnostic and Statistical Manual of Mental Disorders: Fourth Edition (DSM-IV)* (Test revision). Washington, D.C.

Archives of General Psychiatry. 1995. June editorial 52: 422–423.

Armstrong, L. 1993. *And They Call It Help: The Psychiatric Policing of America's Children*. New York: Addison-Wesley Publishing Company.

Arnold, L.E. and Jensen, P.S. 1995. "Attention-deficit disorders." In Kaplan, H.I. and Sadock, B. (eds.). *Comprehensive Textbook of Psychiatry VI*. Baltimore: Williams and Wilkins. 2295–2310

Aune, B. 1983. *Metaphysics*. Minneapolis: University of Minnesota Press.

Baldwin, S. 1999. "Applied behavior analysis in the treatment of ADHD: A review and rapprochement." *Ethical Human Sciences and Services* 1(1): 35–59.

Barkley, R. 1995. "Are behavior modifying drugs overprescribed for America's school children? No: Critics claims are not based on medical reality." *Insight* magazine. In: *New York Times*, August 14, 1995. 18-21.

Barkley, R. 1998a. "ADHD, Ritalin, and conspiracies: Talking back to Peter Breggin. Book review to CHADD." Found on www.chadd.org/Russ-review.htm. May 23, 1998. See Joan Ryan, C.H.A.D.D. Director of Communications.

Barkley, R. 1998b. *Attention Deficit Hyperactive Disorder: A Handbook for Diagnosis and Treatment*. Second edition. New York: Guilford Press.

Bates, B. 1998. "Medication makes the difference in ADHD children." *Pediatric News* 32(12): 1.

Baughman, F.A. 1996. "Fundamentally flawed." Letter to *Clinical Psychiatry News*. January: 8.

Baughman, F.A. 1997. "The future of mental health: radical changes ahead." *USA Today* magazine. March issue. 60-63.

Baughman, F.A. 1999. Personal correspondence and letters from representatives of the child psychiatry research team at the National Institute of Mental Health (NIMH).

Baughman, Jr., F.A. 1993. "Treatment of attention-deficit hyperactivity disorder." *Journal of the American Medical Association* 269: 2368–2369.

Blakeslee, S. 1997. "Some biologists ask: Are genes everything?" *New York Times*. September 2: B-7.

Breggin, P.R. 1994. *Toxic Psychiatry*. New York: St. Martin's Press.

Breggin, P.R. 1997. *Brain Disabling Treatment In Psychiatry: Drugs, Electroshock, and the Role Of The FDA*. New York: Springer Publishing Co.

Breggin, P.R. 1998. *Talking Back to Ritalin: What Doctors Aren't*

Telling You About Stimulants for Children. Monroe, ME: Common Courage Press.

Breggin, P.R. 1999a. "Psychostimulants in the treatment of children diagnosed with ADHD: Acute risks and psychological effects." *Ethical Human Sciences and Services* 1(1): 13–33.

Breggin, P.R. 1999b. The White House Conference on Mental Health. *International Center for the Study of Psychiatry and Psychology Newsletter*. Spring/Summer issue.

Breggin, PR. 1999c. "Psychostimulants in the treatment of children diagnosed with ADHD: Risks and mechanism of action." *International Journal of Risk and Safety in Medicine* 12(1): 3–35.

Breggin, P.R. 2000a. The White House Conference on Mental Health. *Ethical Human Sciences and Services* 2(1): 1-7.

Breggin, P.R. 2000b. *Reclaiming Our Children: A Healing Solution For a Nation in Crisis*. Cambridge, MA: Perseus Books.

Breggin, P.R. 2000c. "A clinical analysis of the NIMH multi-model treatment study of attention deficit hyperactivity disorder (the MTA Study)." *Ethical Human Sciences and Services* 2 (1): 63–72.

Cantwell, D. 1996. "Attention deficit disorder: A review of the past 10 years." *Journal of the American Academy of Child and Adolescent Psychiatry* 35: 978–987.

Carlson, E., Jacobvitz, D., and Sroufe, L.A. 1995. "A developmental investigation of inattentiveness and hyperactivity." *Child Development* 66: 37–54.

Carter, B., Zelko, F., Oas, P., and Waltonen, S. 1990. "ADHD children and clinical controls on the Kaufman Assessment Battery for Children (KABC)." *Journal of Psychoeducational Assessment* 8: 155–164.

Chowdhupry, A.R. and Chattopadbyay, P.K. 1995. "Attention deficit disorder in hyperactive children: An overview." *Social Science International* 11(1–2): 34–43.

Christansen, R.C. and Tueth, M.J. 1998. "Pharmaceutical companies and academic departments of psychiatry: A call for ethics education." *Academic Psychiatry* 22: 135–137.

DeGrandpre, R. 1999. *Ritalin Nation: Rapid-Fire Culture and the Transformation of Human Consciousness*. New York: W.W. Norton and Company, Inc.

DeGrandpre, R. 2000. "ADHD: Serious psychiatric problem or all-American cop-out?" *Cerebrum*, Summer 2(3): 12-39.

Diller, L. H. 1998. *Running On Ritalin: A Physician Reflects on Children, Society, and Performance in a Pill*. New York: Bantam Books.

Drug Enforcement Administration (DEA). 1995. "Methylphenidate: A background paper." Washington, DC: Drug and Chemical Evaluation Section.

Drug Enforcement Administration (DEA). 1996. "Conference report: Stimulant use in the treatment of ADHD." December 10–12. Washington, DC: U.S. Department of Justice.

Education Reporter. 1999. "School board passes resolution warning about Ritalin." St. Louis, MO: Eagle Forum and Legal Defense Fund. December (107): 1-2.

Fantino, E., Case, D., Oas, P. "Observing by humans not maintained by 'bad news'." Paper Presented at the 1981 annual convention of the Eastern Psychological Association.

Faraone, S.V. 1996 "Genetic influence on parent-reported attention-related problems in a Norwegian general population twin sample." *Journal of the American Academy of Child & Adolescent Psychiatry* 35: 596-598.

Faraone, S.V. and Beiderman, J. 2000. "Nature, nurture and attention deficit hyperactivity disorder." *Developmental Review* 20: 568-581.

Fisher, S. and Greenberg, R. (eds.) 1997. *From Placebo to Panacea:*

Putting Psychiatric Drugs to the Test. New York: John Wiley and Sons, Inc.

Gadow, K.D. 1985. "Relative efficacy of pharmacological, behavioral, and combination treatments for enhancing academic performance." *Clinical Psychology Review* 5: 513-533.

Gjone, H. Stevenson, J., and Sundet, J.M. 1996. "Genetic influence on parent-reported attention-related problems in a Norwegian general population twin sample." *Journal of the American Academy of Child and Adolescent Psychiatry* 35(5) 588-596.

Goodman, R. and Stevenson, J. 1989. "A twin study of hyperactivity—II. The aetiological roles of genes, family relationships, and perinatal adversity." *Journal of Child Psychology and Psychiatry* 30: 691–709.

Grinfeld M.J. 1998. "Psychoactive medication and kids: new initiative launched." *Psychiatric Times* 15: 69.

Haddad, P. and Garralda, M. 1992. "Hyperactive syndrome and disruptive early experiences." *British Journal of Psychiatry* 161: 700–703.

Hales, R. and Yudofsky, S.C., eds. 1999. *American Psychiatric Press Textbook of Psychiatry: Third Edition.* Washington, D.C.: American Psychiatric Publishing, Inc.

Hancock, L. 1996. "Why do schools flunk biology?" *Newsweek*. February 19: 58–61.

Harris, J.R. 1998. "The nurture assumption: why children turn out the way they do." *Touchstone*. New York: Simon & Schuster, Inc.

Hechtman, L. (ed.). 1996. *Attention-Deficit/Hyperactivity Disorder: Do They Grow Out of It? Long-Term Outcomes of Childhood Disorders*. Washington, DC: American Psychiatric Press. 17–38.

Hechtman, L. 1994. "Genetic and neurobiological aspects of attention deficit hyperactive disorder: A review." *Journal of Psychiatric Neuroscience* 19(3): 193–201.

Hoagwood, K., Kelleher, K., and Feil, M. 2000. "Treatment services for children with ADHD: A national perspective." *Journal of the American Academy of Child and Adolescent Psychiatry* 39(2): 198–206.

Hooper, S.R. and Tramontana, M.G. 1997. *Advances in Clinical Child Psychology*, Volume 19. Ollendick, Thomas H. and Prinz, Ronald J. (eds.). New York: Plenum Press.

Hubbard, R. and Wald, E. 1993. *Exploding the Gene Myth*. Boston: Beacon Press.

International Narcotics Control Board (INCB). 1999. *INCB Annual Report, Release No. 4*. February 23. United Nations Information Service.

Jacobs, D. 1999. "A close and critical examination of how psychopharmacology research is conducted." *The Journal of Mind and Behavior* 20: 311-350.

Jacobs, J. 1998. "Biases in reporting of ADHD." *Journal of the American Academy of Child and Adolescent Psychiatry* 37: 1009-1010.

Jacovitz, D., Scrouge, A., Stewart, M., Leffert, N. 1990. "Treatment of attentional and hyperactivity problems in children with sympathomimetic drugs: a comprehensive review." *Journal of the American Academy of Child and Adolescent Psychiatry* 29: 5, 677-688.

Jadad, Alejandro R., Booker, Lynda, Gauld, Mary, Kakuma, Ritsuko, Boyle, Michael, Cunningham, Charles E., Kim, Marie, Schachar, Russell. 1999. "The treatment of attention deficit hyperactivity disorder: An annotated bibliography and critical appraisal of published systematic reviews and metaanalyses." *Canadian Journal of Psychiatry* 44(10): 1025.

Johnson, P. 2000. Colorado State Board of Education, 2nd Congressional District. Broomfield, CO.

Joseph, J. 2000. "Not in their genes: A critical view of the genetics of attention deficit hyperactivity disorder." *Developmental Review* 20(4): 539-567.

Journal Watch Psychiatry. 1999. Publication of the Massachusetts Medical Society. Volume 5(11): 85-92. November

Kagan, J. 1965. "Impulsive and reflective children: Significance of conceptual tempo." In: Krumboltz, J.D. (ed.). *Learning and the Educational Process*. Chicago: Rand McNally.

Kagan, J. "The Matching Familiar Figures Test." Available from Jerome Kagan, Department of Psychology and Social Relations, Harvard University, Boston, Massachusetts.

Kagan, J., Rosman, B., Day, D., Albert, J., and Phillips, W. 1964. "Information processing in the child: Significance of analytic and reflective attitudes." *Psychological Monographs* 78(1, 578).

Kendall, P.C. and Braswell, L. 1993. *Cognitive Behavioral Therapy for Impulsive Children*. Second edition. New York: Gilford Press.

Knapp, M. 1997. "Economic evaluation and interventions for children and adolescents with mental health problems." *Journal of Child Psychology and Psychiatry* 38: 3–25.

Kohn, A. 1989. "Suffer the restless children." *The Atlantic Monthly*. November: 90–98.

LeFever, G.B., Morrow, A.L., and Dawson, K.V. 1999. "The extent of drug therapy for attention deficit hyperactivity disorder and our children in public schools." *American Journal of Public Health* 89: 1359–1364.

Lipman, A.J. and Kendall, P.C. 1992. "Drugs and psychotherapy: Comparisons, contrasts, and conclusions." *Applied and Preventive Psychology* 1: 141–148.

Lux, K. 1999. "The failure of the modern experiment and the use of psychotropic drugs." *Ethical Human Sciences and Services* 1(3): 271–275.

Mandelkern, M. 1999. "Manufacturer Support and Outcome." *Journal of Clinical Psychiatry*, February 60(2): 122-123.

Marinoff, L. 1999. *Plato not Prozac - Applying Philosophy to Everyday*

Problems. New York: Harper Collins Publishers, Inc.

McCubbin, M. and Cohen, D. 1999. "Empirical, ethical, and political perspectives on the use of methylphenidate." *Ethical Human Sciences and Services* 1(3): 81–101.

McGuinness, D. 1989. "Attention deficit disorder: The emperor's new clothes, animal 'pharm' and other fiction." In: Fisher, S. and Greenberg, R.P. (eds.). 1989 *The Limits of Biological Treatments for Psychological Distress*. Hillsdale, NJ: Lawrence Erlbaum Associates. 151–188.

McGinis, J. 1997. "Attention deficit disorder." The Wall Street Journal. September 18, 1997. A14.

Millar, T. 1994. *The Omnipotent Child: Third Edition*. Vancouver B.C.: Palmer Press.

Millar, T. 1997. *The Myth of Attention Deficit Disorder*. Vancouver B.C.: Palmer Press.

Morrell, A. 1998. "Attention deficit disorder and its relationship to narcissistic pathology." In: Beron P. (ed.). *Narcissistic Disorders in Children and Adolescents*. New Jersey: Jason Aronson, Inc. 127-149.

MTA Cooperative Group. 1999a. "A 14-month randomized clinical trial of treatment strategies for attention-deficit/hyperactivity disorder." *Archives of General Psychiatry* 56: 1073–1086.

MTA Cooperative Group. 1999b. "Moderators and mediators of treatment response for children with attention-deficit/hyperactivity disorder: the multimodal treatment study of children with attention-deficit/hyperactivity disorder." *Archives of General Psychiatry* 56: 1088–1996.

Munsinger, H. 1975. *Fundamentals of Child Development*. Second edition. New York: Holt, Rinehart and Winston.

National Institutes of Health (NIH). 1998. "Diagnosis and treatment of attention deficit hyperactivity disorder: Program and abstracts." HIH Consensus Development Conference. Rockville,

MD. 2-3.

Novartis Pharmaceuticals. 1997. "Patient Information" brochure. Available from the manufacturer. East Hanover, New Jersey.

Oas, P. 1983. "Impulsive behavior and assessment of impulsivity with hospitalized adolescents." *Psychological Reports* 53: 754–766.

Oas, P. 1984a. "Validity of the Draw-A-Person and Bender Gestalt tests as measure of impulsivity with adolescents." *Journal of Consulting and Clinical Psychology* 52: 1011–1019.

Oas, P. 1984b. "An investigation of the clinical validity of Kagan's Matching Familiar Figures Test with hospitalized adolescents." *Educational and Psychological Research* 4: 177–183.

Oas, P. 1985a. "The psychological assessment of impulsivity: A review." *Journal of Psychoeducational Assessment* 3: 141–156.

Oas, P. 1985b. "Impulsivity and delinquent behavior among incarcerated adolescents." *Journal of Clinical Psychology* 41: 422–424.

Oas, P. 1985c. "Clinical utility of an index of impulsivity on the Draw-A-Person Test." *Perceptual and Motor Skills* 60: 310.

Olsen, S., Bates, J.E., and Bayles, K. 1990. "Early antecedents of childhood impulsivity: The role of parent-child interaction, cognitive competence, and temperament." *Journal of Abnormal Child Psychology* 18(3): 317–334.

Parry, S. 1998. *ADHD: A Market Based Affliction?* Unpublished manuscript.

Perry, B.D. 1998. "Anxiety disorders." In: Coffey, C.E. and Brumback, R.A. (eds.). *Textbook Of Pediatric Neuropsychiatry*. Washington, D.C.: American Psychiatric Press. 579–594.

Pert, C. 1997. Capitol Hill Hearing Testimony: House Appropriations, Labor, Health, and Human Services. November 5.

Physician's Desk Reference. 1998. Montvale, New Jersey: Medical

Economics Company 2078-2079.

Rapoport, J.L., Buchsbaum, M.S. et al. 1980 "Dextroamphetamine: Its cognitive and behavioral effects in normal and hyperactive boys and normal men." *Archives of General Psychiatry* 37: 933-943.

Rapoport, Judith L., Buchsbaum, Monte S., et al. 1978. "Dextroamphetamine: Cognitive and behavioral effects in normal prepubertal boys." *Science* 199: 560–563.

Rappley, M.D., Gardiner J.C., Mullan, P.B., Wang. J., and Alvarez, F.J. 1998. "Psychotropic medications in children ages 1 to 3 with ADHD." Paper presented at Pediatric Academic Societies Meeting (Joint Specialties and Themes: Behavioral Pediatrics), May 4, New Orleans, La.

Rappley, M.D., Mullan, P.B., Alvarez, F.J., Eneli, I.U., Wang, J., and Gardiner, J.C. 1999. "Diagnosis of attention deficit hyperactivity disorder and use of psychotropic medication in very young children." *Archives of Pediatrics and Adolescent Medicine* 153(10): 1039.

Reason, B. 1999. "ADHD: A psychological response to an evolving concept." *Journal of Learning Disabilities* 32(1): 85.

Rosemond, J. 1993. *Making the Terrible Two's Terrific*. Kansas City, Kansas: Andrews McNeel Publishing.

Ross, C.A. and Pam, A. 1995. *Pseudoscience in Biological Psychiatry: Blaming the Body*. New York: John Wiley and Sons, Inc.

Ruff, H.A. and Rothbart. 1996. *Attention in Early Development: Themes and Variations*. New York: Oxford University Press.

Runnheim, V.A. 1996. "Medicating students with emotional and behavioral disorders in ADHD: A state survey." *Behavioral Disorders* 21(4): 306–314.

Russell, J. 1997. "The pill that teachers push." *Good Housekeeping*. December 1997. 110-118, 196-200.

Schulz, K. Himelstein, J. Halperin, J. and Newcom, J. 2000. "Neurobiological models of attention deficit hyperactivity disorder: A brief review of the empirical evidence." *CNS Spectrums* 5(6): 34-44.

Seligman, M. 2000. "Positive psychology." *American Psychologist* 55(1): 5–14.

Shaya, J., Windell, J., and Gilbert, H. 1999. *What You Need To Know About Ritalin: Get the Facts About the Most Prescribed Pill for Attention Deficit Disorder*. New York: Bantam Books.

Skinner, B.F. 1993. *Science and Human Behavior*. New York: Macmillan Publishing Company.

State, M.W., Lombroso, P.J., Pauls, D.L., and Leckman, J.F. 2000. "The genetics of childhood psychiatric disorders: A decade of progress." *Journal of the American Academy of Child and Adolescent Psychiatry* 39(8): 946-962.

Stein, David B. 1999. *Ritalin is Not the Answer. A Drug Free, Practical Program for Children Diagnosed with ADD or ADHD*. San Francisco, CA: Jossey-Bass Publishers.

Suddath, R.L. 1990. "Anatomical abnormalities in the brains of monozygotic twins discordant for schizophrenia." *New England Journal of Medicine* 48: 357-361.

Swanson, J., McBurnett, T., Wigal, T., Pfiffner, L., Lerner, M., Williams, L., Christian, D., Tamm, L., Willcutt, E., Crowley, K., Clevenger, W., Khouzam, N., Woo, C., Crinella, F., and Fisher, T. 1993. "Effect of stimulant medication on children with attention deficit disorder: A 'review of reviews.' " *Exceptional Children* 60(2): 154–162.

Szasz, T.S. 1961. *The Myth of Mental Illness: Foundations of a Theory of Personal Conduct*. New York: Hoeber-Harper.

Thompson, R.A. and Nelson, C.A. 2001. "Developmental science and the media: Early brain development." *American Psychologist* 56(1):5-15.

Vaidya, C.J., Austin, G., Kirkorian, G., Ridlehubert, H.W., Desmond, J.E., Glover, G.H., and Gabrieli, J.D.E. 1998. "Selective effects of methylphenidate in attention deficit hyperactivity disorder: A functional magnetic resonance study." *Proceedings of the National Academy of Sciences* 95(24): 14494–99.

Valenstein, E.S. 1998. *Blaming the Brain - The Truth About Drugs and Mental Health*. New York: The Free Press.

Valentine, M.R. 1988. *How To Deal With Difficult Discipline Problems: A Family-Systems Approach*. Dubuque, Iowa: Kendall/Hunt Publishing Company.

Volkow, N.D., Ding, Y.S., Fowler, J.S., Wang, G.J., Logan, J., Gatley, J.S., Dewey, S., Ashby, C., Lieberman, J., Hitzemann, R., and Wolf, A.P. 1995. "Is methylphenidate like cocaine? Studies on their pharmacokinetics and distribution in the human brain." *Archives of General Psychiatry* 52 (June): 456–463.

Volkow, N.D. Wang, G.J., Fowler, J.S., Logan, J., Gatley, S.J., Dewey, S.L. and P., Hitzemann, P., Chen, A.D., Dewey, S.L., and Pappas, N. 1997. "Decreased striatal dopaminergic responsiveness in detoxified cocaine-dependent subjects." *Nature* 386: 830–833.

Volkow. N.D. 1999. "Association of methylphenidate-induced craving with changes in right striato-orbitofrontal metabolism in cocaine abusers: Implications in addiction." *American Journal of Psychiatry* 156: 19–26.

Walker, Sidney III, M.D. 1996. *A Dose of Sanity*. New York: John Wiley and Sons, Inc.

Wazana, A. 2000. "Physicians and the pharmaceutical industry: Is a gift ever just a gift?" *Journal of the American Medical Association* 283(3): 373–380.

Wender, P.H. 1995. *Attention Deficit Hyperactivity Disorder in Adults*. New York: Oxford University Press.

Whalen, C.K. and Henker, B. 1997. "Stimulant pharmacotherapy for attention deficit hyperactivity disorders: An analysis of progress, problems, and prospects." In: Fisher, S. and Greenberg, R.P. (eds.). *From Placebo to Panacea: Putting Psychotropic Drugs to the*

Test. New York: Wiley. 323–347.

Wray, H. 1997. "How the nature-nurture debate shapes public policy - And our view of ourselves." *U.S. News and World Report*. April 21, 1997. 45-51.

Zachary, G.P. 1997. "Male order: boys used to be boys, but do some now see boyhood as a malady?" *The Wall Street Journal*. May 2. A1.

Zametkin, A.J., Nordahl, T.E., Gross, M., King, A.C., Semple, W.E., Rumsey, J., Hamburger, S., and Cohen, R.M. 1990. "Cerebral glucose metabolism in adults with hyperactivity of childhood onset." *New England Journal of Medicine* 323: 1361–1366.

Zarin, D., Suarez, A.P., Pincus, H.A., Kupercanin, E., and Zito, J.M. 1998. "Clinical and treatment characteristics of children with attention deficit hyperactivity disorder in pediatric practice." *Journal of the American Academy of Child and Adolescent Psychiatry* 37(12): 1262–1270.

Zito, J.M., Safer, D.J., dos Reis, S., Gardner, J.F., Boles, M. and Lynch, F. 2000. "Trends in the prescribing of psychotropic medications to preschoolers." *Journal of the American Medical Association* 283(8): 1–16.